Geeks

&

Geezers

Geeks

&

Geezers

How Era, Values, and Defining
Moments Shape Leaders

Warren G. Bennis

Robert J. Thomas

HARVARD BUSINESS SCHOOL PRESS

Boston, Massachusetts

Requests for permission to use or reproduce material from this book should be directed to permissions@hbsp.harvard.edu, or mailed to Permissions, Harvard Business School Publishing, 60 Harvard Way, Boston, Massachusetts 02163.

Library of Congress Cataloging-in-Publication Data

Bennis, Warren G.
  Geeks and geezers : how era, values, and defining moments shape leaders / Warren G. Bennis, Robert J. Thomas.
    p. cm.
Includes bibliographical references and index.
  ISBN 1-57851-582-3 (alk. paper)
  1. Leadership. 2. Executive ability. 3. Executives—Biography. I. Thomas, Robert J., 1952- II. Title.
  HD57.7 .B4578 2002
  303.3'4—dc21

                                            2002004910

The paper used in this publication meets the requirements of the American National Standard for Permanence of Paper for Publications and Documents in Libraries and Archives Z39.48–1992.

To Grace, Rosanna, and Alyssa

CONTENTS

W E W E R E D R A W N to thinking and then ultimately writing about geeks and geezers from very different starting points. Coauthoring a book isn't quite like synchronized swimming. It's more like gaining perspective and depth through incongruity. Through writing and arguing in what seemed like endless and percussive to-and-froing, helped along by endless and percussive e-mailing, we strove to achieve a coherent voice. But first, to honor the differences, we thought it only appropriate to offer our individual reflections on this project and its meaning.

From Warren Bennis: That I would eventually write a book on geeks and geezers will come as a surprise to no one. I have almost always allowed personal experience to peek through in my work, however distanced and objective the surface. When I was a younger man, I never thought of myself as a geek. At the time, the word did not mean a nerdy, technologically sophisticated person in the mold of Bill Gates. A geek was a carnival performer who made his living biting the heads off live chickens—and that's still the only definition you'll find in any but the most recent dictionaries. Although I did not know I was a geek (in the current sense) when I was one, I am acutely aware that, in the eyes of the world at least, I am now a full-fledged geezer—born in 1925 and seasoned on the now almost mythological battlefields of World War II. I will spare you a protracted discussion of such autumnal truths as the fact that all of us stay 16 in our hearts and, at some point, look into the mirror and wonder who that white-haired person is. If you are my age, you already know that; if you are younger, you will learn it soon enough. But I will tell you a little about how this book came to be.

Information guru and intellectual matchmaker Richard Saul Wurman called me several years ago and asked if I would speak at one of his annual TED conferences. As you probably know, TED stands for Technology, Entertainment, and Design. And every year Richard gathers a group of people he finds interesting—and a somewhat larger group of people willing to pay to be around that core group—for three days of observation, prognostication, idea swapping, food, drink, bombast, and schmoozing. "This year, Warren," Richard told me, "we're only inviting speakers seventy years and older and thirty years and younger." I thought Richard was onto something here, as he usually is. A project began to coalesce around the idea that geeks and geezers have valuable but different things to contribute to almost any discussion. Both groups know things that all of us should know.

Much of the appeal of this project-in-the-making was the opportunity to delve deeper into the thought world of geeks, the cohort born around 1970 and after that has preoccupied the media, and especially the business media, for almost a decade. Nothing gives me greater joy than learning something new, and I realized there was a gap in my understanding of the views and values of these geeks and their younger brothers and sisters—the first generation, as Bob and I say in our book, to have grown up virtual, visual, and digital.

The realization that there were holes in my understanding of what motivated and moved the young was most vivid in the classroom. For several years, University of Southern California president Steve Sample and I have cotaught a course on leadership at USC. Every year, we invite Michael Dukakis to speak to our class. As all of you who are over 30 know, Dukakis was the Democratic candidate for president in 1988 and a distinguished governor of Massachusetts. But our students, bright as they are, tend to look back blankly when we excitedly announce that Mike will be speaking to them. The few who recognized his name knew it from reruns of the "Saturday Night Live" parody of Mike's ill-fated campaign tank ride, in which comic Jon Lovitz impersonated him. I know that most of our students, however bright and well informed, tend to think of Vietnam, Watergate, and other land-marks of the last forty years as distant, even ancient history. But I am always a little shaken that so many have never heard of Michael Dukakis, whose run for president seems so recent to me.

Besides wanting to probe the minds and experiences of geeks, I was also eager to learn more about my fellow geezers. As a life-long student of leadership, I've always been fascinated both by those who become leaders and those who don't. Just as intriguing as great leaders, in many ways, are those gifted people who some-how get stuck and never manage to actualize their talents. The frustration of talent and the embitterment that usually follows is one of the saddest phenomena I know—and one of the most instructive. Moreover, I have always been interested in develop-ment, even before I took up the subject of becoming a leader. In 1956, my first published paper was about group development. By 1964, I was writing about organizational development, and about the correspondences between healthy individuals and healthy organ-izations. Growth and change have been the major themes of my entire professional life.

Not surprisingly, in recent years, I've grown ever more curious as to why some people seem to age and others do not. We all know people who hit 70, say, and suddenly look and act old, with all the diminution and loss that term has traditionally implied. And yet, thankfully, there are others who manage to stay forever young, whatever their chronological age. To some extent, the difference is probably genetic. But it is not only that. There is some other quality that allows a Rudolph Serkin to dare, at the age of 80, to master an entirely new, modern repertoire when he might so eas-ily have continued to perform more traditional music forever. Or take 76-year-old film director Robert Altman, who keeps reinventing himself with such films as his 2001 *Gosford Park*. People like Serkin and Altman, or dancer Martha Graham (who transcended the blow of being fired by her own troupe and reinvented herself as a crowd-pleasing lecturer/performer), or Winston Churchill (who, one of his biographers wrote, jay-walked his way through life until he was 66), have a secret that all of us would do well to discover. They are proof, heartening to see, that growing old does not preclude living life with enormous brio.

Meanwhile, at another TED Conference, I ran into old friend Phil Slater, the gifted sociologist and writer. I told him about the geeks and geezers project and talked excitedly about a couple of great geezers I had interviewed and the almost magical quality of excitement and engagement they radiated. "Neoteny," Phil said. "It's called *neoteny*." Later, I asked him to elaborate, and he answered with an autobiographical e-mail. "I often feel isolated because so many of the people I know," he wrote, "have 'settled' in some way. The world has jelled for them—closed. It no longer has the sense of possibility that it had for many of us as children. The neoteny I was talking about has to do with the fact that some of us have kept that sense of possibility and wonder alive. I'm not sure what all is involved in that or why it happens, but I see it in a lot of successful people (it's why they're so much more fun to talk to about ideas than academics are), and it's very meaningful to me." Much of this book is about that remarkable quality.

In the fall of 1999, I was in London, having lunch with Tom Davenport, a partner at Accenture and author. With Tom was colleague Bob Thomas. A Northwestern-trained sociologist and former MIT professor, Bob told me of his deep interest in the impact that era has on leadership. It was clear that Bob and I were covering some of the same ground and moving in the same direction, and I realized, almost at once, what a find he was and what a fine collaborator he would be. Again and again, he sharpened my thinking and we pulled from each other insights neither of us would have had working alone. He was an intellectual sparring partner of the first order and a generous soul. The truth is that I am not sure, and don't think Bob is either, about who came up with this or that idea.

As the best projects always do, this one turned out to be even more interesting than we thought it would be. You will discover all that we did in the pages that lie ahead, but let me make one point at the outset. It soon became clear that we were studying not just lifetime leadership, but how people learn to live well decade after decade. The more we talked to our geeks and geezers, the more apparent it became that this was a story not just about leadership development but about human development. At some point, we realized that the two are inexplicably intertwined, that the very factors that make a person a great leader are the ones that make him or her a successful, healthy human being. It was a thrilling "eureka!" moment. Want to find out how able a leader an individual will be? Look at how he or she deals with being imprisoned, as our geezer Sidney Rittenberg was. (Rittenberg was imprisoned for sixteen years by the Chinese Communists.) The leadership of a Rittenberg or a Nelson Mandela doesn't magically appear when the spotlight is turned upon them. It was there, waiting to be expressed, long before the prison doors swung open, thanks to the qualities and almost alchemical process that we will describe in depth in the coming chapters.

As we have talked to different audiences about geeks and geezers, we find that certain of our key ideas excite them most. The crucible—the transformational experience that all our leaders have had—is one. Era is another. David Gergen recently asked me to talk about the book at the Center for Public Leadership at Harvard's John F. Kennedy School of Government, which Gergen heads. Afterwards, he excitedly covered the blackboard with notes on the impact of different eras on recent history. Leaders like Truman, he pointed out, were shaped by World War I, the growth of big business, and the idea of the melting pot. Subsequent leaders such as JFK and George Herbert Walker Bush were formed in the crucible of World War II and came of age in a nation unified by its fight for its very survival. A distinguished commentator and advisor to four presidents, Gergen then spoke movingly of his own generation. Like Gergen, former President Clinton, Vice President Al Gore, and the younger President Bush were all children of the 1960s, who grew up in a nation divided over the Vietnam War, in a nation of divided families. None of the presidents served in that war. Most poignantly, Gergen contrasted their formative era of fragmentation and national discord with that of earlier eras that seemed to share a common purpose and simpler values. I can only hope that all our readers respond to our study of geeks and geezers as thoughtfully, enthusiastically, and personally as Gergen did.

From Bob Thomas: A few years back, while watching choreographer Twyla Tharp lead a class with her students at City Center in New York, I learned something important about practice. I am not a dancer, but I sensed that Tharp's students were struggling to understand what she wanted them to do with a particularly complex combination of moves (or phrases, in the grammar of dance). Marveling at the back-and-forth interrogation, the demonstration and mimicking of physical gestures, and the quiet but earnest pleading to "do it my way" taking place between choreographer and dancers, I realized that in that moment, the distinction between practice and performance hardly existed at all. They were performing while they practiced. I could easily imagine them onstage a few weeks hence *practicing while they performed.*

Watching Twyla Tharp and her dancers, I was reminded that business managers routinely complain that they don't have time to "practice" being leaders. They have to perform all the time. Each in his or her own way genuinely wants to improve as a leader but doesn't know how. They enroll in leadership workshops, pay for coaching sessions, and pack off to weekend retreats, but the lessons just don't seem to stick. From my perch in the balcony that night in Manhattan, I realized that the problem wasn't that managers couldn't learn to lead. What they lacked was a concept of practice. To be more precise, they needed a way to practice *while* they performed.

After creating an experimental curriculum for the Leaders for Manufacturing Program at MIT—a curriculum that included dance lessons for engineers—I left the university to see what I could learn about leadership practice by watching effective leaders perform. Along the way I had the great fortune to work with business, union, and political leaders in the United States, Venezuela, Jamaica, India, Germany, and Japan. And the effective ones, the ones who truly engaged their people as what Warren calls "intimate allies," were the men and women who practiced leading every moment of every day. They recognized no distinction between work and life. They were the same people on the job and off. They used every situation they encountered as a practice field and they mined every experience for insight about themselves and the people and the world around them. Leading is not only what they did, it was who they were.

Which brings me to geeks and geezers. Warren and I first talked about studying older and younger leaders only a few days after a former student of mine called to say he was departing a very senior position in a conventional bricks-and-mortar manufacturing firm for the wilds of online retailing. I understood his sense of adventure, but what I didn't get was why he would walk away from almost certain success. Sighing, he warned me, "White guys in their fifties and sixties just don't get it." I hastened to remind him that I wasn't 50 yet. But, reluctantly, I had to admit that I didn't get it either. This project with Warren gave me the opportunity to see if I could get it. I think now that I do.

Warren G. Bennis
Santa Monica, CA

Robert J. Thomas
Brookline, MA

ACKNOWLEDGMENTS

W<small>HAT A PLEASURE</small> it is to acknowledge, to show apprecia-
tion, to express thanks. Especially when you know that this
book would never have seen the (de)light of day if it hadn't been for
the dozens of individuals and groups and institutions who served,
one way or another, as cheerleaders, supporters, midwives, producers, critics, advisors, subjects, facilitators, sponsors, connectors,
listeners, reviewers, and so on. One of our favorite book dedica-
tions goes simply "*Without whom* . . . ." Well, there are many
"whoms" to whom we want to express our gratitude. In fact, we
wish we could roll the credits the way films and TV shows do,
with all the subtleties that the insiders understand, like best boy
and gaffer and ADs, caterers, creators, executive and coproducers, and so forth. In a way, this book was developed like a film or
TV show.

First of all, we have a producer, Tom Davenport, a distinguished
author and director of Accenture's Institute for Strategic Change.
His support and uncurbed enthusiasm, plus his ability to provide
the generous financial and intellectual resources, were critical.
You couldn't want for a better maestro than Tom. Along the way,
he enrolled a few coproducers from within Accenture. Mike May,
along with John Rollins and Chris Burrows, recognized the value
of investigating generational differences in leadership style. They

gave us the stage, the cameras, the crews, and the wherewithal for this project. Inspirational leaders all.

Then we had a "High Concept": comparing the Digital Set with the Analog Set, the 70-years-plus leaders with the 30-year-old leaders, the geeks and geezers. That was handed to us by Richard Saul Wurman, the whiz, master impresario, stand-up creative genius who convened one of his TED conferences in Monterey in 2000, where the only invited speakers were 70 years and older and 30 years and younger. He had two titles for this conference, Geeks and Geezers, which he allowed us to steal, and the less catchy but delightful Will and Still.

We also assembled a terrific cast who agreed to work without fees and showed up on time. Robert Altman, who was himself shooting *Gosford Park* in England and was unable to join us, couldn't have done better. We're talking about our "subjects," really our coinvestigators, our geeks and geezers, who dropped what they were doing to appear with us. Though not as well known as Maggie Smith or Michael Gambon, Muriel Siebert and Sidney Harman have as much presence on life's stage as any of Altman's cast. Just about every idea in this book came from one of our stars.

We also had a number of consultants and advisors, paid and unpaid. The Harvard Business School Press sent out advance copies for "peer review" to a slew of people who were paid equity fees, which means enough to pay for postage and make copies at Kinko's. So we can't credit them publicly though we have an idea or two about who they are. Not naming them is much the same as when Jack Nicholson or Meryl Streep makes one of their cameo appearances and goes unlisted when the credits are rolled. So thanks to all those behind-the-scenes folks who gave us, sight unseen, such terrific suggestions.

We also profited enormously from the tips, admonitions, and wisdom given us by a wide number of scholarly friends. We want to single out a number of them—a banquet of "whoms."

First, to get even close to meeting our own expectations of what this book could be, the counsel of Robert Butler and James

Birren, the two pioneers and virtual founders of the field of gerontology, was essential. We also want to thank Edward Schneider and Caleb Finch of USC's School of Gerontology; Howard Gardner, Roger Gould, Hal Leavitt, Gil Levin, Mel Roman, and George Vaillant, all more knowledgeable about the field of human development than we are and, just as important, such generous minds. We also have to add—are bursting with pride to add—Will Bennis, working on his Ph.D. in human development at the University of Chicago. He has served us well, like a mentor. (He also interviewed his dad for this book.)

Others whose ideas have advanced our thinking are Nitin Nohria, David Gergen, Rosabeth Moss Kanter, Jean Lipman-Blumen, Lester Thurow, Paul Lagace, Jan Houbolt, and Barbara Kellerman. Barbara deserves major kudos for weighing in with her intellectual heft from the very beginning of our work. She also has the useful talent for asking the annoyingly right questions.

We also want to single out the redoubtable Horace Deets, who only recently stepped down from a long run of success as executive director of the AARP. Horace, to be fair, was concerned about our title. We reassured him that the geeks wouldn't mind at all. His wisdom and his leadership of AARP serve as an exemplar of all we've been writing about here.

To continue the movie metaphor, we've had some "sneak previews" at various venues over the past two years or so. The truth is that neither of us has ever written a book quite like this. We wanted to present our central ideas to live audiences before committing our words to paper. So we opened in Monterey, California, at the TED conference in February, 2001; in March at USC's Provost Writers Series; in August at Gil Levin's Cape Cod Institute; in October at Harvard to the Kennedy School's Center for Public Leadership; and in November to Boston University's School of Management, the Linkage Global Leadership Institute, and the Leadership and Behavioral Sciences faculty at West Point. These "sneak previews" were, for us, like focus groups, helping us clarify our ideas and learn, as they say in Hollywood, what's hot and what's not.

Because we videotaped nearly all of our interviews, we had several production teams. Marina Kalb and Michael Kirk, professional filmmakers, gave advice and access to their stellar video crew contacts. Cameraman Jim Sicile recorded many of our interviews and added great fun to the task. Cary Benjamin and his team at T&R Productions helped us capture vivid moments from our tapes so that we could study them closely and illustrate our key concepts. Cherie Potts transcribed every word from our interviews and, though distant from the process, offered valuable insights.

Jim Wilson, whom Bob refers to as a "literary green beret," stepped in with brief but valuable bursts of editorial support. Alex Beal, Diana Moscone, Alyssa Bottone, Fiona Heldt, and Lawrence Tu also pitched in and gave us a hand when needed. Again, Accenture's Institute for Strategic Change gave them the license and the time to help out.

The Los Angeles crew consisted of three indispensable and longtime associates of Warren's. His assistant at USC, Marie Christian, has an eye for error and a loupe glass for judgment. Geoff Keighley, a former student, is one of our geeks and a techie entrepreneur. (You'll see in the book how he started his business at the advanced age of 14.) He translated almost 90 percent of the presentation material from video, interviews into PowerPoint, which at times seems like his, and other geeks', first language. And thanks and hugs to Warren's longtime friend and coauthor, Pat Biederman, a *Los Angeles Times* reporter. Her fine editorial acumen is noticeable throughout.

Our research crew, from both coasts, consisted of, again, Geoff Keighley, Chris Maguire, and Margaret Stergios who contributed valuable insights on the world according to geeks, as well as expert research assistance.

USC's Marshall School of Business Administration has helped us in so many ways—a venue for our interviews, secretarial and administrative support, and wise counsel from Tom Cummings and Randy Westerfield. USC's president and provost, Steve Sample and Lloyd Armstrong, respectively and respectfully, are owed a deep bow of thanks.

Let us now praise some Remarkable Women: Carol Franco, the guiding light of the Harvard Business School Press, who, in her "neotenic" way (in order to understand the fullness of that compliment, read chapter 1) recruited us, encouraged us, made us feel terrific and loved throughout a rather long gestation period, and gave us access to her incredibly able staff, from the designers to the marketers to all those who can bring a superb product to market. Finally, we have been blessed to have the editorial advice of two of the most prized editors at the Press, Hollis Heimbouch and Suzanne Rotondo. The artist Georges Braque famously said that "the only thing that matters in art, can't be explained." Well, you can say the same thing about editing. It is an art form, and Hollis and Suzanne are virtuosi to whom we shout BRAVA! BRAVA! And yes, without whom . . . without whom this book would not make us as proud as we are.

Between us we have published some thirty books. Neither of us has ever worked with a crew as supportive, as competent, as trustworthy, and as caring as the Press's staff.

Finally, a personal note. Rosanna Hertz has proven (again) her extraordinary talent as Bob's critic, commentator, editor, cheerleader, logician, and confidante—all while chairing an academic department and moonlighting as a building contractor.

A final, final personal note. Grace Gabe, who has been kept busy enough writing her own book, has been supportive and loving and more than a little helpful throughout the two and a half years it has taken her husband, Warren, to coauthor this book. Somehow or another, she was able to endure the ups-and-downs of her husband's obsessiveness with something approaching equanimity. That's devotion.

Growing up, Harry Truman never thought of himself as a leader, nor did anyone else. With "eyeglasses thick as the bottom of a Coke bottle," historian David McCullough writes, Truman couldn't try out for school sports and mostly stayed home, working the farm, reading, or playing the piano.[1] Friends thought he was a sissy, and so did he. When he graduated high school, his family had run into hard times and he remained on the farm, the only president of the 20th century who never went to college.

But the course of his life changed forever when, at the age of 33, he signed up for the Army to fight in World War I. He was shipped off to France as the head of an artillery battery, and there for the first time in his life he was forced to lead men through moments of mortal danger. His initial test came on a rainy night in the Vosges Mountains. The Germans had dropped an artillery barrage close by, and his troops, panicked that they were being gassed, ran for it. In the frenzy, Truman's horse fell over on him and he was nearly crushed. Writes McCullough: "Out from under, seeing the others all running, he just stood there, locked in place, and called them back using every form of profanity he'd ever heard . . . shaming his men back to do what they were supposed to do." They regrouped, got through the night and many of them eventually got home safely. Throughout the rest of their lives they were loyal to Harry Truman, their leader who refused to back down in the face of his own fear.

According to McCullough, Truman discovered two vitally important things about himself that night. First, that he had plain physical courage; second, that he was good at leading people. "He liked it and he had learned that courage is contagious. If the leader shows courage, others get the idea." Adds McCullough:

"And the war was the crucible."[2]

The crucible—how important that was in Truman's life and how central it is to the story that Warren Bennis and Robert Thomas tell in the pages of this illuminating book. Time and again, as we see here, leaders both young and old have emerged as they have faced tough—even harrowing—challenges, stiffened, adapted, and eventually have come through on the other end. Business leader Sidney Rittenberg survived sixteen years in a Chinese prison; journalist Mike Wallace was seared by the accidental death of a beloved son; Muriel Siebert, the first woman to own a seat on the New York Stock Exchange, had to endure years of prejudice against women executives; Nathaniel Jones had to struggle against intense racial prejudice; the noted public servant John Gardner grew up quickly as a Marine officer responsible for the welfare of his men; Wendy Kopp went through numerous trials building Teach For America, the organization she founded just after she left college. These are engrossing stories and show, as the authors say, that if a person can not only survive but create positive meaning out of such experiences, she or he can grow into a durable, effective leader. Like Harry Truman, they embarked upon "a hero's journey," conquered their dragon, and returned in a state transformed.

At least one national organization has formally embraced the idea of a crucible as a training ground for future leaders—and has found that it works. In the mid-1990s, with the economy booming and labor markets tight, the U.S. military services were struggling to meet their enlistment goals. The Army, Navy, and Air Force decided to make their services more appealing by improving living conditions, allowing recruits more time with their families, and the like. The Marine Corps went the other way: It toughened up. General Charles Krulak, the Commandant, introduced "The Crucible" to Marine training—an incredibly grueling fifty-four straight hours of live fire exercises, long marches, and sleep deprivation at the end of basic training. After climbing the final hill in this test, recruits are presented with the eagle, globe, and anchor emblem. And with that, finally, they are Marines. Potential recruits rallied to the idea and the corps, alone among the services, saw its enlistments shoot up. Not long ago, Seth Moulton, a young Harvard graduate who signed up to become a Marine officer in the wake of September 11, returned to Cambridge after ten weeks in Quantico and related to me that the idea of the "Crucible" has now been incorporated throughout training. For Seth, and for others like him, the Marines provide a welcome path toward positions of leadership.

Yet the very fact that a crucible appears so central to the development of leaders raises questions for which we do not yet have full answers. Why, for example, do some people find times of testing and adversity a great source of strength while others become discouraged and shrivel up? If you are running an organization, how can you spot those who will succeed and those who will fail when trials come? As a mentor or teacher, how can you help someone prepare for difficulties that may lie ahead? What counsel can you offer?

History has certainly made it clear that adversity often separates winners from losers. In his work *Greatness: Who Makes History and Why*, Dean Keith Simonton argues, "To achieve success of the highest order, a person may have to suffer first."[3] He points out that orphanhood, especially the tragic early loss of the mother, has been conducive to the development of political reformers, philosophers, and religious figures in modern times. Some 63 percent of British prime ministers between Wellington and Chamberlain suffered early parental loss. However, two other groups, juvenile delinquents and depressive or suicidal psychiatric patients, show orphanhood rates similar to those of the eminent public figures. In other words, some rise from their crucible but others certainly fall. Why?

This portrait of "geeks and geezers" also suggests that for women, it appears more difficult to gain the developmental experiences that help to shape leaders. Most of the men here were thrown into a cauldron and grew by learning how to adapt. Once in the crucible, they discovered qualities in themselves that then propelled them forward as leaders. That was certainly true of John Gardner and others who signed up for the military and were soon thrust into positions of leadership. It was true as well for Vernon Jordan, who signed up for a job in a white home and suddenly found himself struggling to assert his own identity.

But the women who appear in these pages had to strike out on their own—they had to assert a significant degree of leadership *before* they found their crucible. Tara Church formed a national organization as a young girl; Wendy Kopp formed a national organization as a young woman. Elizabeth Kao worked her way up through Ford Motor Company. The women who emerge as leaders are far more the product of self-selection than are the men. What that suggests is that many other women have not had the same opportunities as men to discover their leadership potential and thus remain hidden. In all likelihood, that means the pool of women who develop into leaders remains smaller than the pool of men. And thus we face the inevitable question: Having encouraged greater educational opportunities for women in past years—and seeing how rapidly they have succeeded—how do we encourage greater leadership opportunities for women too? We know that women make excellent leaders; that debate is largely over. Now we must face the challenge of ensuring equal opportunities for development.

This book also points to an issue about male development. Among men in the older generation of leaders, World War II was often the defining moment in their lives. As horrific as war might be, the years in uniform transformed many of those who survived. But in today's context, even with a war on terrorism underway, the percentage of young men who serve in the military has shrunk dramatically. For kids coming out of rural America or off the streets of inner cities, that ladder up has largely disappeared. It is worth asking what, if anything, has taken its place as a crucible. If you come from a well-heeled family, a chance for travel and adventure is still there, but for millions of young men today— especially those who are black, Hispanic, or from rural areas— horizons can be extremely limited. We don't offer the kind of democratizing experiences that we had in the days of a military draft when, as it was said, a Saltonstall took orders from a Polish kid from Brooklyn.

Reading this excellent book, I couldn't help but wonder how America could provide more inspiring opportunities for the potential leaders of the next generation, both men and women. Is national service an answer? Wouldn't it help if we created a national culture in which the young were expected to give at least a year back to the country? Wouldn't many of them find their own crucible? This is not the time or place to explore those questions, but perhaps as you join Warren Bennis and Robert Thomas in their reflections on "geeks and geezers," you might think of ways we could inspire leaders to arise from the next generation. We need them.

David Gergen
Cambridge, MA

Geeks

&

Geezers

ONE

Leading and Learning for a Lifetime

IN ONE of his best-known essays, E. B. White, sage of the *New Yorker*, wrote: "There is a bright future for complexity, what with one thing always leading to another." As he so often does, White wraps a profound idea in the simplest of packages—not surprising for a man who dared to use the word *crepuscular* in a children's book and created an eight-legged thought leader in Charlotte, the oracular arachnid of *Charlotte's Web*.[1]

What White distills in his observation about complexity is a basic truth about leading and learning—about the way we discover something valuable, give it a tug, and find that it inevitably leads us to another discovery and then another. The ability to learn is a defining characteristic of being human; the ability to continue learning is an essential skill of leadership. When leaders lose that ability, they inevitably falter. When any of us lose that ability, we no longer grow.

At its heart, this is a book about leadership and learning and about the almost magical process by which some people succeed, however they define success, not just once but again and again. It is a book about cross-generational leadership that looks, for the first time, at two groups of leaders—our youngest and our oldest, the geeks and the geezers—and asks them to tell us what they have discovered about leading, learning, and living well in the course of their very different lives and times. It is a book that grapples with such compelling questions as why some people are able to extract wisdom from experience, however harsh, and others are not. It asks successful geeks to share the secrets of their youthful triumphs and distinguished geezers to tell us how they continue to stay active and engaged despite the changes wrought by age. What all these people have to say is so important, so useful, that we believe it will help readers find their own best strategies for leading and learning, not just for a time but for a lifetime.

The predictable format for such a book would simply be to ask well-known leaders to share their secrets—that is what most books on leadership do. But this book goes beyond personal revelations to postulate a theory of leadership. An important part of that theory is recognition of the role that distinctive periods in history play in producing leaders. All of us come of age in a particular place and time—an era—that shapes us in large and small ways. Although we are rarely aware of this influence from day to day, our era determines choices both mundane and profound, from the music we prefer to the things that we long for, the things we take for granted, and much of the emotional coloration of our lives. Our geeks and geezers are no exception. In the two chapters that follow, we will attempt to place our geeks (most of them under 30) and our geezers (most in their 70s and 80s) in the historical contexts that produced them. We know that this is a little like trying to write a twelve-page version of the collected works of Shakespeare. But in order to understand what our participants have to say, it is important to keep in mind some of the major forces that shaped them.

"I'll have someone from my generation get in touch
with someone from your generation."

The world has changed more in the eighty or so years since our oldest leaders were born than it had in the previous millennium. To name a single remarkable difference, the world is now "wired," a term that would have made little or no sense to the man in the street of 1920. We believe that leadership in this world of ever-accelerating change requires both the wisdom of our elders and the insights of younger people who, despite their youth, have already demonstrated their leadership ability. We often hear of the impact that 70 million baby boomers, born between 1946 and 1963, are having on every aspect of our lives, including the global economy. Too little has been said about the way the world is being transformed daily by another, even larger, cohort—the 85 million people who are now between the ages of 2 and 22.

This is the first cohort to grow up visual, virtual, and digital, and we ignore it at our peril.

A New Model of Leadership

As we explain in the preface, this book started out as a study of both young and old leaders and how era influences leadership, but it evolved into something more. As a result of our research for the book, we have developed a theory that describes, we believe for the first time, how leaders come to be. We believe that we have identified the process that allows an individual to undergo testing and to emerge, not just stronger, but equipped with the tools he or she needs both to lead and to learn. It is a model that explains how individuals make meaning out of often difficult events—we call them *crucibles*—and how that process of "meaning-making" both galvanizes individuals and gives them their distinctive voice. That model (shown in figure 1-1) describes a powerful chain reaction of change and growth.

Figure 1-1 **Our Leadership Development Model**

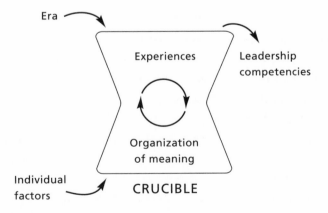

Much of this book is devoted to explicating that model and showing how it is reflected in the development of leaders of all ages. The process we will explore is one that allowed Nelson Mandela not simply to survive, but to emerge from twenty-seven years in a South African prison as the most powerful moral leader since Gandhi. It is the process that forged a Franklin Delano Roosevelt, a Golda Meir, and a Martin Luther King, Jr. It is the process that led one of our geezers, Sidney Rittenberg, to pioneer business ties between the United States and China after spending sixteen years in Chinese prisons during the 1940s and 1950s, and that produced gifted geeks like educational activist Wendy Kopp and serial entrepreneur Michael Klein. Our model explains how leaders develop, in whatever era, and predicts who is likely to become and remain a leader. In the pages that follow, you'll discover why some people are able to lead for a lifetime, while others never seem able to unleash remarkable gifts. You'll see why *learning* to learn is key to becoming a leader. And you'll discover why the factors that produce leaders are the same ones that predict something far more important than professional success: They are the very factors that allow us to live happy, meaningful lives.

Defining Our Terms

When we first began talking about leadership as a lifetime process, we used polite, even euphemistic, terms to describe the two groups that most interested us—youthful leaders who discovered their abilities early and older ones who were able to create leadership roles for themselves decade after decade. (For a complete list of those we studied, see table 1-1 and the brief biographies in appendix A.) At first, we spoke of "younger leaders and mature leaders," of "Greatest Generation leaders and those from Generation X." But as our conversations became more animated and intense, we dropped the polite terms and opted for a more convenient, if less flattering, shorthand. We began referring to our two groups as *geeks* and *geezers*.

Table 1-1 **Geezers and Geeks Interviewed in the Project**

Geezers

Warren G. Bennis	Edwin Guthman	Richard Riordan
John Brademas	Sidney Harman	Sidney Rittenberg
Jack Coleman	Frances Hesselbein	Muriel Siebert
Robert L. Crandall	Dee Hock	Paolo Soleri
Father Robert F. Drinan	Nathaniel R. Jones	Walter Sondheim, Jr.
Robert Galvin	Arthur Levitt, Jr.	Mike Wallace
John Gardner	Elizabeth McCormack	John Wooden
Frank Gehry	Bill Porter	
Don Gevirtz	Ned Regan	

Geeks

Elizabeth Altman	Sky Dayton	Brian Morris
Lorig Charkoudian	Harlan Hugh	Lingyun Shao
Steve Chen	Elizabeth Kao	Young Shin
Tara Church	Geoffrey Keighley	Bridget Smith
Ian Clarke	Michael Klein	Brian Sullivan
Dan Cunningham	Wendy Kopp	Jeff Wilke

Although these terms may seem self-explanatory, let us be precise about them. The geeks whose leadership fascinated us are young (35 and under); most of them are involved in the now troubled but still vital New Economy. In deciding upon our geeks, we looked for outstanding achievement at a notably early age, combined with a thoughtful ability to articulate their experiences, observations, and views. We consciously sought out men and women who had led or even built organizations—having a good idea or a "killer app" alone would not qualify someone for inclusion if they did not also prove themselves capable of leading people.

The geeks in our study are a varied lot. They are the heads of dot-coms and other information-based organizations, including Sky Dayton, founder of Earthlink and Boingo Wireless; chocolatier

Dan Cunningham; and digital iconoclast Ian Clarke, founder of FreeNet. They are accomplished executives in more conventional businesses, like Elizabeth Kao at Ford Motor Company and Elizabeth Altman at Motorola. A few started organizations in order to serve causes dear to them, such as Tara Church, who was an 8-year-old Brownie when she founded the environmental group Tree Musketeers, and Lorig Charkoudian, who founded Baltimore Community Mediation, which helps community members resolve disputes nonviolently. Whether or not they work in the technology sector, they are geeks in the sense of "computer geeks"— young people who have been working with digital technology for as long as they can remember. Theirs is the first cohort to have had computers in elementary school. People with 1s and 0s in their blood, they interact with machines as easily as with other human beings—more easily, critics say.

The leaders we termed *geezers* are the grandparents of our geeks. That's literally true in the case of Bob Galvin, vice chairman of Motorola, who is the grandfather of Brian Sullivan, CEO of Rolling Oaks Enterprises. These geezer men and women (far more of the former than the latter, sad to say) are widely admired for their wisdom and skill. Some are retired, but most continue to lead major corporations and other successful organizations. Reduced to what National Public Radio's David Brancaccio calls "the numbers," our geezers are all 70 and over. When selecting geezers, we were especially interested in people who may have changed arenas but continue to be involved in important work and engaged with the world. The geezers who fascinate us are people like Mel Brooks, who, at 75, launched a new career for himself as a songwriter and won twelve Tonys—the all-time record—for the Broadway show he helped create from his manic film classic *The Producers*. You need only to have seen Brooks giddily accept Tony after Tony during the 2001 telecast of the theatrical awards show to realize that creativity and vitality are functions of factors other than age. Indeed, his strategy for dealing with his age is to ignore it: "I don't look in the mirror and I don't look in the calendar," he has said. Thus, we were intrigued by leaders like Frank

Gehry, designer of the most talked-about building of recent times—the gleaming, undulating Guggenheim Museum in Bilbao, Spain. He turned 70 in 2000 and yet continues to play the ice hockey he has loved since he was a boy in Toronto. Other geezers include Visa International founder Dee Hock, former Securities and Exchange Commission head Arthur Levitt, Jr., former Los Angeles mayor Richard Riordan (who once played ice hockey against Gehry), Wall Street pioneer Muriel Siebert, CBS News editor and correspondent Mike Wallace, and UCLA basketball coach John Wooden.

Recording Leadership in Images and Stories

We wanted our leaders to share their experiences because we know the power of stories and their ability to convey complex, nuanced information. We wanted the leaders to tell us, in their own words, the aspirations, drives, and events that shaped them, the lessons they learned, and the insights they gained. At the same time, we wanted to collect data systematically so we could see what patterns emerged when that data was analyzed. In order to collect information that could be collated and compared, we asked each person the same set of questions, but we also gave them the opportunity to make any observations they deemed relevant. We decided to videotape the interviews whenever possible, because we knew taping would preserve a wealth of information that no transcript could capture, from body language to subtle shifts in emphasis and energy. Watching the tapes later did indeed remind us of the catch in a voice that marked some unforgettable event, the brio with which they talked about their work, the visible anguish that some showed as they remembered instances of tragedy and loss, the tenderness with which mentors were recalled. We reasoned that this mixed-media approach would give us the best of both worlds— empirical data that would allow us to draw valid conclusions and an invaluable archive of images and stories of leadership that would long linger in the reader's, and the viewer's, mind.[2]

After several refinements and considerable tweaking, the questionnaire we administered asked such key questions as: What were the defining moments in your life? How did you get from here to there? How do you define success? How did you define it at 30? What makes you happy? What role has failure played in your life?

Remember that the questionnaire (appendix B) was only a starting point, albeit a critical one. Some of the most telling information emerged late in these interviews of two hours or more, after the subjects, assuming the interviews were essentially over, had forgotten the video camera and relaxed.

The resulting 43 interviews with leaders ranging in age from 21 to 93 are powerful in their insight and candor. As we asked our subjects to think deeply about their lives, we realized that we were really writing collaborative autobiographies. We were asking them to reveal how they saw themselves, to share the lives they had both lived in reality and constructed in their own minds. In a sense, we were asking them to tell us who *they* believed themselves to be. Insights from the interviews will form the core of the next two chapters. Chapter 2 elaborates our arguments about the importance of era and values in shaping leaders while focusing on the formative period for our geezers, 1945–1954. We turn to the geeks in chapter 3 and learn what leadership, success, and fulfillment look like to those who came of age in the years 1991–2000.

Although Bennis and Biederman have proclaimed the death of the Great Man (and Woman) in *Organizing Genius: The Secrets of Creative Collaboration* and elsewhere, this project literally focused the camera on the person at the top and gave only fleeting acknowledgment to the network of people who make any complex organization or enterprise a success.[3] We made a deliberate decision to emphasize the leader rather than his or her inevitable partner, the group, because we had so much that is new and important to say about leaders. However, it is still true that "None of us is as smart as all of us" and that one is usually too small a number for greatness. In virtually every case, our leaders, both young and old, are successes because of their ability to identify, sustain, and inspire other talented people.

Our goal in structuring this book is to convey the excitement we experienced as we listened to our geeks and geezers and began to formulate our underlying model of leadership development (see figure 1-1). In the brief sections that follow we post a road map of the main elements of that model and how they emerged, beginning with the impact of era on leadership aspirations and behaviors, exploring the power of crucible experiences in shaping leadership values and character, and closing with an introduction to the distinctive capacities of men and women who lead for a lifetime.

The Impact of Era

Era is an aspect of leadership that has not received the attention it deserves, given how profoundly it shapes individual leaders. We see era as important, not because it defines individuals, but because it presents them with a shared history and culture and a specific arena in which to act. As Oliver Wendell Holmes observed: "A great man represents a strategic point in the campaign of history, and part of his greatness consists of his being there."

Eras are quite different from generations, those periods that occur every eighteen years or so and define all who fall within them. The eras we are talking about are characterized by defining events, and may occur every twenty years or less. Members of the same generation may react quite differently to the opportunities and challenges each new era creates. Certainly the era in which we grew into maturity remains an important force throughout our lives. But in the course of a long life, we experience many eras. The last twenty years, marked by the advent of the Internet and the end of the Cold War, can be seen as one coherent era. It is not yet clear whether the terrorist attacks of 2001 marked the end of that era of American hegemony and unprecedented prosperity.

Analog is the umbrella word that best describes the era that produced our older leaders, *digital* the term that characterizes the era of our younger leaders (see table 1-2). Many of the older subjects mastered such analog tools as the slide rule, an object as foreign to most of our geeks as a record album or a typewriter. An in-depth analysis of the pervasive impact of digital technology is beyond the scope of this book. But it is obvious that the computer and the Internet have had a profound effect on those who grew up with them (as well as on those who didn't), from shrinking the size of their mental globe (almost anyone on the planet is only a keystroke away) to providing instant access to information that may or may not be accurate. One of the geeks we interviewed, Ian Clarke, is so much a child of the digital age that he says he can't imagine what he would have become without the Internet—perhaps, he says with a shudder, "an accountant and miserable."

What are some relevant characteristics of the world in which our older leaders were formed? How is the world different today? The analog world was one that valued linear narrative and thinking. It believed in organizational hierarchy and chain of command. The digital world is nonlinear and has ditched the corporate pyramid for the flat organization. To use psychologist Karl Weick's insightful metaphors, the world born during the Depression and World War II could be understood using a map. To make sense of

---

Table 1-2 **Era-Based Differences**

Analog	Digital
Linear	Nonlinear
Maps	Compasses
Mechanics	Living systems
COP (command, order, predict)	ACE (align, create, empower)
Experience	Beginner's mind
Conventional warfare	Terrorism and cyberwarfare
Specialist	Deep generalist

the Wild West of the digital world requires a compass. As Weick explains: "Maps, by definition, can help only in known worlds—worlds that have been charted before. Compasses are helpful when you are not sure where you are and can get only a general sense of direction."[4]

Whether or not their parents owned TV sets, geeks are children of television. The widespread introduction of television in the early 1950s was a watershed in leadership as in so many other things, from family life to the arts. The people born and raised *after* that world-changing event are forever marked by their ease in processing a tsunami of visual information at breakneck speed. Today's ordinary American is exposed to more novel visual images in a single day than the average Victorian experienced in a lifetime. You need only look at how differently the generations learned fundamentals. As children, geeks didn't learn the alphabet in a measured singsong, as did virtually everybody over 50. They shouted it out, one letter chasing another, as they learned to do on *Sesame Street*. They never slogged through grammar lessons of heartbreaking tedium. Instead, "Conjunction Junction" and the other upbeat lessons of *Schoolhouse Rock* were set to jazz riffs, tunes still sung aloud on social occasions in Silicon Valley and other capitals of the New Economy.

Even the controlling metaphors of the two eras differ. Older leaders were trained to think of the world in Newtonian, mechanical terms. Younger ones tend to look at the world in terms of living organisms and biological systems that are constantly changing and evolving. Men and women over 70 experienced—and understood—conventional warfare, as horrible as it is. Men and women under the age of 30 know only the random nightmare of terrorism and the ever-present threat of biological and cyberwarfare. Experience was valued by an earlier era—implicit in the idea of seniority is the notion that valuable lessons are learned only over time. Fifty years ago, the leader was expected to have survived a period of testing and was thought to be the better for it. Winston Churchill expressed this attitude when he said: "I rate the capacity of man by, first, courage and ability; and second, real experience under fire." Today's society tends to value what Zen Buddhists call the "beginner's mind." It implies fresh insight unfettered by experience. In this more contemporary view, the compelling idea is the novel one at an angle to conventional wisdom, itself a phrase that implies a regressive reliance on the status quo. Perhaps no one articulated the nature of the beginner's mind better than the composer Berlioz when he said of Saint-Saëns: "He knows everything. All he lacks is inexperience." Yesterday's leaders were specialists who sought and trusted answers. Today's tend to be generalists who know they need to ask the right questions.

What are the implications of era for the way our geeks and geezers think about the leader's role? We found three key differences between geeks and geezers when we compared their hopes and aspirations at the same age (roughly 25–30). First, geeks have bigger and more ambitious goals than geezers did at the same age; they aspire to "change the world" and "make history," whereas geezers were concerned with "making a living." Second, geeks place far more emphasis on achieving balance in their work, family, and personal lives than did geezers at a comparable age. And third, geeks are far less likely than geezers to have heroes or to have had their image of a successful leader shaped by a hero. No issue or attitude divided the two groups more dramatically than that of the drive among geeks for work-life balance, which we will explore in much greater detail in chapter 3. Taken as a whole, these differences, we suggest, are directly linked to the eras in which each group matured as leaders.

We also uncovered convergences in worldview among these older and younger leaders. For example, both groups are avid learners: They are captivated by learning new things and are constantly on the lookout for ways to enhance their ability to learn. These geeks and geezers are also alike in that they forever strain to transcend limits, whether those limits are individual, like strength or learning ability, or institutional, like racial and/or sexual discrimination.

However, the most dramatic tie connecting the men and women we interviewed was their common experience of events that transformed their behavior and self-understanding. The discovery of this common tie propelled us from a simple, albeit very interesting, comparison of geeks and geezers to a much deeper investigation of how people become leaders.

The Power of the Crucible

We found that every leader in our study, young or old, had undergone at least one intense, transformational experience. That transformational experience was at the very heart of becoming a leader. The descriptive term we found ourselves using is *crucible*. The *American Heritage Dictionary* defines crucible as "a place, time or situation characterized by the confluence of powerful intellectual, social, economic or political forces; a severe test of patience or belief; a vessel for melting material at high temperatures." A crucible was the vessel in which medieval alchemists attempted to turn base metals into gold. That the alchemists inevitably failed in their audacious attempts doesn't negate the power of the crucible as a metaphor for the circumstances that cause an individual to be utterly transformed.

Because crucibles are so critical, we will devote all of chapter 4 to them. As the event or relationship that forged a leader, the crucible is at the center of our model (see figure 1-1). The crucibles that produced our leaders were as varied as being mentored, mastering a martial art, climbing a mountain, and losing an election. Sometimes the crucible was an upbeat, even joyous experience. Video game expert Geoff Keighley, 21, remembers his whole life changing in second grade, when he made a magician's table out of a microwave box, put on a top hat, and performed a dazzling magic trick at a friend's birthday party. "It set me apart," said Keighley, remembering how the wonder and respect of his young audience filled him with a sense of power and uniqueness.

Sometimes the crucible is a tragedy. Pioneering television journalist Mike Wallace was uncertain whether he should give up his prestigious, well-paying job with a local station and try for a network slot when, in 1962, his oldest son, Peter, a student at Yale, fell off a mountain while on vacation in Greece. Two weeks after Peter disappeared, Wallace found the boy's body. "That was really the turning point when I said, 'To hell with it,' " Wallace recalled. "I'm going to quit everything and do what I want to do now."

One of the harshest crucibles in our study was that which shaped businessman Sidney Rittenberg, 79. In China in 1949 Rittenberg was jailed as a spy by former friends in Chairman Mao's government. He spent sixteen years in prison, the first year in solitary confinement and total darkness except when he was being interrogated and the remaining fifteen years in permanent lighting without the benefit of darkness. He emerged certain that absolutely nothing in professional life could break him.

The crucible need not be a horrendous ordeal. Motorola vice president Liz Altman, 34, didn't go to prison. But she was utterly transformed by the year she spent in a Sony factory in Japan, finding her way in an alien corporate world whose broad cultural differences—particularly its emphasis on groups over individuals—were both a shock and a challenge to a young American woman. Muriel Siebert, the first woman to own a seat on the New York Stock Exchange, was shaped by the Wall Street of the 1950s and '60s, an arena so sexist that she couldn't get a job as a stockbroker until she took her first name off her resume and substituted a genderless initial. Thrust into the alpha-male world of Wall Street, Siebert wasn't broken or defeated. Instead, she emerged stronger, more focused, and determined to change the status quo that excluded her.

World War II was a crucible for almost all our older male leaders, many of whom were transformed by the terrible responsibility of leading other men into battle. The war was also a crucible for many in that it allowed them to recognize for the first time that they had the ability and desire to lead. Common Cause founder John Gardner, 89, identified his arduous training as a Marine as the crucible in which his leadership abilities emerged. "Some qualities were there waiting for life to pull those things out of me," he told us, with characteristic eloquence. The battlefield and basic training are recognized rites of passage after which people are different; their values and the way they see the world are for-ever changed. The quality of that change is captured in the obser-vation by many Vietnam veterans that the war was in Techni-color, but everything before and after was in black and white.

Mentor-protégé relationships constitute another, very power-ful, kind of crucible. The importance of mentoring has become almost a cliché of management literature, but, as we will show in chapter 4, mentoring shares with other crucibles a powerful process of learning, adaptation, and transformation that is intensely indi-vidual, whether it occurs in a family or an organization. Consider, for example, Michael Klein, a young man who made millions in Southern California real estate while still in his teens. As Klein told us, his mentor was his grandfather, Max S. Klein, who cre-ated the paint-by-numbers fad that swept the United States in the 1950s and '60s.[5] Klein recalled that he was only 4 or 5 years old when his grandfather approached him and offered to share his expertise in business. The grandfather noted that Michael's father and aunt—Max's only children—had no interest in business and told young Michael, "You're never going to get any money from me . . . but I'll tell you anything you want to know and teach you anything that you want to learn from me." We learn from stories like Klein's that teaching is never solely the function of the men-tor. The protégé can also be a teacher, a guide to the mindset and skills of a younger generation that allows the mentor to continue learning and to cope more successfully with inexorable change.

Whether the crucible experience is an apprenticeship, an ordeal, or some combination of both, we came to think of it much like the hero's journey that lies at the heart of every myth, from *The Odyssey* to *Erin Brockovich*. It is both an opportunity and a test. It is a defining moment that unleashes abilities, forces crucial choices, and sharpens focus. It teaches a person who he or she is. People can be destroyed by such an experience. But those who are not emerge from it aware of their gifts and goals, ready to seize opportunities and make their future. Whether the crucible was harrowing or not, it is seen by the individual as the turning point that set him or her on the desired, even inevitable, course.

Creating Meaning Out of the Crucible Experience

Leaders create meaning out of events and relationships that devastate nonleaders. Even when battered by experience, leaders do not see themselves as helpless or find themselves paralyzed. They look at the same events that unstring those less capable and fortunate and see something useful, and often a plan of action as well. A powerful example is that of Vernon E. Jordan, civil rights pioneer and presidential advisor. In his 2001 memoir *Vernon Can Read!*, Jordan describes the vicious baiting he received as a young man from his employer, Robert F. Maddox.[6] Jordan served the racist former mayor of Atlanta at dinner, in a white jacket, with a napkin over his arm. He also functioned as Maddox's chauffeur. Whenever Maddox could, he would derisively announce, "Vernon can read!" as if the literacy of a young African American were a source of wonderment. So abused, a lesser man might have allowed Maddox to destroy him. But Jordan wrote his own interpretation of Maddox's sadistic heckling, a tale that empowered Jordan instead of embittering him. When he looked at Maddox through the rear-view mirror, Jordan did not see a powerful member of Georgia's ruling class. He saw a desperate anachronism who lashed out because he knew his time was up. As Jordan writes: "I do not mean just his physical time on earth—but I believed that the 'time' that helped shape him was on its way out. His half-mocking, half-serious comments about my education were the death rattle of his culture. When he saw that I was in the process of crafting a life for myself that would make me a man in some of the same ways he thought of being a man, he was deeply unnerved."[7] The home in which Jordan was a servant was the crucible in which, consciously or not, Jordan imbued Maddox's cruelty with redemptive meaning. And thus are leaders made.

Nelson Mandela used his powerful character and imagination to thwart his jailers' attempts to dehumanize him. "If I had not been in prison," he told Oprah Winfrey in an interview in 2001, "I would not have been able to achieve the most difficult task in life, and that is changing yourself." Notice how Mandela made lemonade from the most bitter of lemons. He saw himself not as a passive victim—someone who was imprisoned by others—but as an individual who had been "in prison." Instead of allowing his jailers to define him, Mandela fashioned a heroic identity for himself—one that inspired millions in Africa and elsewhere and was instrumental in ending apartheid and creating a new, multicultural South Africa. For Mandela, the crucible was both an external reality and something he created in the process of imbuing it with meaning.

Much of the leadership literature focuses on the traits or habits of leaders. In fact, every individual has a unique set of obstacles as well as assets that he or she brings to the table. Whether the bar is poverty, insecurity based on some physical attribute (Mike Wallace's teenage acne), or ethnic or racial discrimination (architect Frank Gehry was so troubled by widespread anti-Semitism that he changed the family name from Goldberg shortly before his first child was born), everybody enters the lists with a burden, a perceived reason for not succeeding. Ford Motor Company executive (and geek) Elizabeth Kao expressed the concept well when she said: "Everybody has their own wall to climb." One of the key differences between leaders and nonleaders, we found, is the ability of leaders to transmogrify even the negatives in their lives into something that serves them. For leaders, the uses of adversity are genuinely sweet.

What Makes a Leader

An important part of our leadership model is what lies on the other side of the crucible—the qualities that define lifetime leaders and learners, qualities that we will discuss at length in chapters 4 and 5. The one key asset all our leaders share, whether young or old, is their adaptive capacity. The ability to process new experiences, to find their meaning and to integrate them into one's life, is the signature skill of leaders and, indeed, of anyone who finds ways to live fully and well. Of all our subjects, none showed greater adaptive capacity than Sidney Rittenberg. Thrown into a Chinese jail, confined in a pitch-dark cell without any explanation, Rittenberg did not rail or panic. You wonder what you would do in such dreadful circumstances, if you would be able to come out whole. Within minutes, Rittenberg recalled matter-of-factly, a stanza of verse popped into his mind, four lines read to him as a little boy:

> *They drew a circle that shut me out,*
> *Heretic, rebel, a thing to flout.*
> *But love and I had the wit to win.*
> *We drew a circle that took them in.*[8]

That bit of verse (adapted from "Outwitted" by Edwin Markham) was the key to Rittenberg's survival. "My God," he thought to himself, "there's my strategy. There's my program." Evidence of the power of Rittenberg's ability to adapt and survive is Rittenberg Associates, the consulting firm that he founded and continues to run, which helps American companies do business with the Chinese. As his example so vividly reminds us, bitterness is maladaptive.

Optimism is an element of what health psychologists term *hardiness*, a rubric for the cluster of qualities that equip people for serial success (see chapter 5 for a fuller discussion of these qualities). Tenacity and self-confidence are others. But leaders share less obvious assets as well. As Saul Bellow says of the character very like himself in his novel *Ravelstein*, they are all "first-class noticers." Being a first-class noticer allows you to recognize talent, identify opportunities, and avoid pitfalls. Leaders who succeed again and again are geniuses at grasping context. This is one of those characteristics, like taste, that is difficult to break down into its component parts. But the ability to weigh a welter of factors, some as subtle as how very different groups of people will interpret a gesture, is one of the hallmarks of a true leader.

One of the best ways to define good leadership is to study bad leaders. Although we explore this approach at length in chapter 5, a single instance is instructive here: Shakespeare's tragic Roman general Coriolanus. A great warrior, a man with a strong moral compass, Coriolanus has only one flaw—his utter inability to reach out to the people of Rome and engage them in his vision. Rereading the play in the context of leadership, we couldn't help thinking of Coriolanus's mother, Volumnia, as the ancient Roman equivalent of an executive coach saddled with a particularly thick-headed client. Talk to the people, she encourages her son again and again. But Coriolanus doesn't get it. He fails to grasp the expectations of the people or how they will respond to his aloofness. He is convinced that reaching out to the populace would be a form of pandering, that it would require him to sacrifice his integrity.

Finally, before we conclude this overview of our leadership model, we need to say something more about one of the most exciting ideas to emerge from our research. We discovered that every one of our geezers who continues to play a leadership role has one quality of overriding importance: neoteny. The dictionary defines *neoteny*, a zoological term, as "the retention of youthful qualities by adults." Neoteny is more than retaining a youthful appearance, although that is often part of it. Neoteny is the retention of all those wonderful qualities that we associate with youth: curiosity, playfulness, eagerness, fearlessness, warmth, energy. Unlike those defeated by time and age, our geezers have remained much like our geeks—open, willing to take risks, hungry for knowledge and experience, courageous, eager to see what the new day brings. Time and loss steal the zest from the unlucky, and leave them looking longingly at the past. Neoteny is a metaphor for the quality—the gift—that keeps the fortunate of whatever age focused on all the marvelous undiscovered things to come. Frank Gehry designs buildings that make architects half his age gasp with envy. Neoteny is what makes him lace up his skates and whirl around the ice rink, while visionary buildings come to life and dance inside his head.

Walt Disney, of all people, did a good job of describing his own neoteny. "People who have worked with me say I am 'innocence in action,'" he wrote. "They say I have the innocence and unselfconsciousness of a child. Maybe I have. I still look at the world with uncontaminated wonder." [9]

The capacity for "uncontaminated wonder," ultimately, is what distinguishes the successful from the ordinary, the happily engaged players of whatever era from the chronically disappointed and malcontent. Therein lies a lesson for geeks, geezers, and the sea of people who fall in between. In the next two chapters we'll see how two profoundly different eras influenced the motivations, values, and aspirations of these men and women.

Geezers

The Era of Limits

WHAT DIFFERENCE does it make in the life and mind of a leader to have been born in 1925 versus 1975? How is it different being bright, ambitious, and 25 in 1950 versus the year 2000? We are not social historians, so we don't intend to rerender history in a novel or comprehensive way. We seek instead to offer a series of snapshots that capture the zeitgeist, or spirit of the times, of the formative years of each group. Then we will show how the two groups actually lived and learned in this broader, yet defining, context.

To accomplish this, we first look at each group's coming-of-age years: 1945–1954 for the geezers, and 1991–2000 for the geeks. In this chapter, we explore the milieu in which geezers stretched their wings as young adults and as leaders. We refer to this time as the Era of Limits. Chapter 3 provides a parallel look at geeks during what we label the Era of Options.

The Era of Limits: 1945–1954

Victory in World War II inspired careful optimism in Americans, but this momentary elation was tainted by the revelation of Nazi death camps and by the awful responsibility of owning the nuclear bomb. The nation grew tense as the "hot" war in Europe and the Pacific gave way to an ideological Cold War between democratic and communist states. In the summer of 1950, North Korean Communist armies, sponsored by China and the Soviet Union, marched into South Korea. President Harry S. Truman captured the tenor of the nation in this diary entry: "It looks like World War III is here—but we must meet whatever comes, and we will."[1] The U.S. rapidly cemented its role as a global superpower, not only through the "police action" to contain communism in Korea, but also through the rebuilding of Europe under the Marshall Plan and the extended occupation of Japan (1945–1952). Like a child who suddenly gets his wish, America struggled throughout the era to understand and define its role on the world stage.

Postwar youth had to live with the psychic repercussions of World War II for the rest of their lives. In August 1946, John Hersey's short novel *Hiroshima* filled an entire issue of the *New Yorker* magazine, and it later became a national best-seller. Describing the human cost of a nuclear blast through the eyes of a few ordinary people, the novel awakened many Americans to the real dangers of the dawning nuclear age. In 1948, Norman Mailer's *The Naked and the Dead* revisited the tragedy of war in all its gritty detail. While they would not soon forget the lessons of the war, young Americans were anxious to mend their psychic and bodily wounds. They remembered their parents' struggles during the Depression years of their childhood, yet they found jobs in a booming economy, bought suburban houses, and filled newly built schools with their children.

Former GIs and their families were poised to inherit the earth—but the earth was trembling beneath their feet. Even in a time that *Life* magazine calls "the most bountiful period in U.S.

history," suburbanites installed backyard bomb shelters.[2] Indeed, fear of communism "in our own backyards" grew into a national obsession. In 1947 a group of Hollywood screenwriters were interrogated, jailed for a year, and blacklisted. A few years later, the executions of Julius and Ethel Rosenberg for espionage riveted the attention of the nation and much of the world. Pope Pius XII advised clemency, and French philosopher Jean-Paul Sartre called the execution "a legal lynching that cover[s] a whole nation in blood."[3] The freedom for which young Americans fought seemed threatened from all sides.

During this time the GI Bill inundated universities with students who had suffered the horrors of war. Young people bought suburban homes and enjoyed a material comfort unknown to their Depression-era parents. The Kinsey Reports on human sexuality alternately scandalized and titillated the nation. A young writer named Jack Kerouac was literally on the road, taking notes on experiences that would galvanize the Beat movement a few years later; schoolchildren listened to Bert, an amiable animated turtle, who sang "Duck and Cover" to instruct them in the event of nuclear catastrophe. Consider it a time of stability with limitations: The promise of abundance and progress was shadowed by the fear of nuclear destruction or another stock market disaster.

Big Business and the Organization Man

Big business flourished in the decade following World War II, and the companies that anticipated the transition to a postwar economy did best of all. Legions of veterans and their young families moved west across the country in search of the good jobs in the burgeoning aerospace sector, or north to new jobs offered by industrial expansion. When one of us (Warren) first began teaching at MIT's Sloan School of Management, every student was a married white male in his mid-thirties. The only "minority" students were Canadian, and almost no students were from small

entrepreneurial companies. Instead, seats in business schools like
Sloan were filled by men from corporate behemoths.

These behemoths—including automakers General Motors and
Ford, consumer durables manufacturers like General Electric and
Westinghouse, and the beneficiaries of the Cold War arms race,
such as Lockheed and General Dynamics—grew at breakneck speed
to capture dominant positions in their markets. Vertical integration
was the principle strategy as these enormous firms sought to protect
their core assets from potentially crippling disruptions in supply.

Business leaders invested tremendous faith in science and technology. After all, advances in nuclear technology, radar, and sonar
research contributed to victory in World War II. After the war, the
sciences continued to blossom: Medical researchers developed syn-
thetic antibiotics, chemists created plastics and pesticides, and
nuclear physicists made progress toward harnessing nuclear energy.
Through technology, an already prosperous America was cata-
pulted to global economic dominance.

With the postwar resurgence in labor unions in key sectors of
the economy, big business meant good jobs with good benefits.
Indeed, thanks to the UAW's success in collective bargaining in this
era, the very concept of employment benefits was born: In many
industries, workers availed themselves of health insurance, pensions, and paid vacations for the first time. Union leaders were
respected for gaining these significant advances in the quality of
life for employees.

One of the most important implications of the growth of the
large-scale business enterprise was the emergence of the "Organization Man" about whom William H. Whyte wrote so incisively
in 1956:

> *They are not the workers, nor are they the white-collar people in*
> *the usual, clerk sense of the word. These people only work for*
> *The Organization. . . . They are the ones of our middle class who*
> *have left home, spiritually as well as physically, to take the vows*
> *of organization life, and it is they who are the mind and soul of*
> *our great self-perpetuating institutions.*[4]

Careers in the era of the Organization Man were imbued with the idea of reciprocal loyalty: of employee to organization and boss and of organization to employee. Hardly paternalistic, big business operated on the basis of engineering models of problem solving and rational calculation, while rewarding commitment and hard work. In many respects, the notion of career was inextricably intertwined with the military experience of chain-of-command and standard operating procedures: Follow the rules and obey authority, and things will work well. When things work well, everyone benefits. In this regime, experience was valued because it implied knowledge. Equally important, however, it demonstrated acceptance of the legitimacy of the rules of the game. There was at root a social contract that tied employer and employee together. The employee, to a certain extent, gave up his individuality for the "brotherhood" of the organization. In reciprocity, the organization guaranteed the employee the "good life" through salary and security.

Racing to the Middle

Demographically and economically, the United States was becoming a middle-class society in this era. Even as economic inequality persisted and racial discrimination in the north began to draw attention, the American Dream took on the flavor of its middle class. America was under the thrall of television; it shaped the way people used their leisure time, got their news, and made sense of the world. Even in its infancy, TV shaped white suburbia's self-image and spotlighted the ideal nuclear family. Whatever the social realities of the time, television consistently portrayed men as breadwinners and women as homemakers. The media acknowledged only heterosexual couples (despite the Kinsey Report's revelations about homosexuality), and gender and race severely limited the future choices of little boys and girls. Of course, reality did not conform to the antiseptic surfaces of television: The roots of feminism and civil rights were spreading underground throughout the fifties. In 1950, a young man named Martin Luther King,

Jr., was reading Ghandi, and in 1955 Eleanor Roosevelt published an article entitled "What Are the Motives for a Woman Working When She Does Not Have to for Income?" Her answer in the article—self-fulfillment—did not fit the typical female stereotype for women in the fifties.[5]

Regardless of these undercurrents of resistance, advertisements for cars, appliances, furniture, and cigarettes featured well-groomed young couples frolicking with their children. Foreshadowing the era of the geeks, advertising began to rival the power of political ideology. How powerful was the entertainment/advertising conglomerate? When Lucille Ball admitted to a journalist in 1953 that she once joined the Communist Party to please her grandfather, her sponsor, Philip Morris, refused to withdraw support from the enormously popular *I Love Lucy* show. America was so enamored of Lucy's ditsy housewife that she was quickly forgiven when Desi Arnaz quipped that the only thing red about Lucy was her hair—and even that was dyed.[6]

Organized religion dominated the moral landscape of postwar America. Though it's impossible to say precisely that Americans of this era were more or less religious than in the era of the geeks, they were certainly more institutional in their worship.[7] Churches sprouted with every new suburban development. The dominant ideology of Christianity encompassed moral life on a national level. The struggle against communism was a biblical battle between good and evil in the minds of most Americans, who were convinced that God was on the side of democracy. In 1950, a former communist "convert" wrote:

Communism is not new. It is, in fact, man's second oldest faith. Its promise was whispered in the first days of creation under the tree of Good and Evil: "Ye shall be as gods." Other ages have had great visions. They have always been different versions of the same vision: the vision of God and man's relationship to God. The communist vision is the vision of man without God.[8]

Americans trusted public institutions, perhaps because of the sacrifices they'd made to preserve them, but also because so many of them had benefited from public works programs as children in the 1930s. The United States, in a very short time, geared up to win a war. Shortly after accomplishing that mission, 2.25 million men and women took advantage of the GI Bill from 1945 to 1954. American leaders wisely created the Marshall Plan and did not dethrone the emperor of Japan. People complained about the government and taxes, but even the conservatives who rewrote New Deal legislation never expressed open contempt for the institutions of government. White, middle-class America favored the new buildings, bright classrooms, and large patches of open space for children to play at suburban public schools. The contrast between the suburbs and cities grew stark as the middle class moved to new developments and bought cars, abandoning public transportation and city schools. With Social Security, the Wagner Act, and the desegregation of the armed forces, the U.S. government set out to redress conditions for the weak and oppressed.

There were real icons in this era, people whom the editors of *Time* magazine called "All purpose heroes . . . who are right and true all the time."[9] Sports heroes like Joe DiMaggio and Stan Musial represented the ideal of American manhood. A handful of movie and television actors, including Jimmy Stewart, John Wayne (both of whom had served in the military), and Lucille Ball, were universally beloved. Political and ideological icons like Franklin and Eleanor Roosevelt, Dwight D. Eisenhower, and Douglas MacArthur were more than celebrities; they commanded respect from wide swaths of the population.

A Bridge across Eras

A core hypothesis of this book is that the era into which we are born has a profound impact on our lives, although we are rarely aware of it day to day. The films that speak to a particular generation are especially telling—reminders of a shared past in which every detail, from clothing styles to common values, reflects a shared identity. What geezer is not moved by Fred Zinnemann's cinematic adaptation of James Jones's tale of America on the brink of war, *From Here to Eternity*? Why do such culturally hip contemporary films as *High Fidelity*, Stephen Frear's portrait of the socially inept and musically obsessed, resonate so strongly with geeks? Each of these films is dense with cultural information fully understood only by people who have been there, done that. But such films also function as windows on eras other than our own, allowing us to bridge—if only for ninety minutes, with a box of popcorn in hand—what Phil Slater calls the "experiential chasms that so often keep generations apart."[10]

One very big consideration shaped our thinking: Any comparison involving attitudes or experiences would have to be "apples and apples," that is, between men and women at the same stages of their lives. To that end, we asked the same questions about each individual's aspirations, worries, and relationships at similar points in their lives. For example, when we asked our subjects to identify "defining moments" in their leadership journey, people often proceeded chronologically, anchoring them in the time (and age) when a defining moment occurred. When geezers identified such a moment between the ages of 25 and 30, we probed with questions that served as the foundation for our comparison. This tactic enabled us to compare and contrast two groups of young people, thus bridging the formative eras for geeks and geezers.

Although we will take up an explicit comparison of the effects of era on each group's aspirations and motivations as leaders in the concluding section of chapter 3, it helps to peek at a few features of the demography of each era to heighten the contrast (see table 2-1).

Geezers at Age 25–30

What were the men and women we interviewed over the age of 70 thinking about when they were 25–30 years old? What impact did

Table 2-1 **Selected Demographic Differences between the Era of Limits and the Era of Options**

	Era of Limits	Era of Options
Average household size	3.37	2.63
% of children living in 2-parent families	86.5%	69.0%
Median age for marriage (male/female)	22/20	27/25
% of female population in labor force	30.9%	59.8%
Life expectancy if born in 1925 versus 1975 (male/female)	66/71	73/79
% of men over 65 still in labor force	47.0%	16.4%

the Era of Limits have on them as individuals and as leaders? Figure 2-1 summarizes key themes that emerged from the interviews with our over-70 leaders. It also highlights the causal relations that people drew as they explained the effect of era on their own lives.

Making a Living

In 1959, the Milton Bradley Company commemorated its hundredth anniversary by introducing what publicists dubbed a "modern" board game, the Game of Life. The game featured a road from high school to retirement, complete with shortcuts and detours, thoroughfares and dead ends. Advertising copy for the game advised players: "Land a great job, get married, and fill up your car with kids! Dodge bad luck and make a buck. End up with the biggest fortune, and you'll retire in style as a winner!"

Figure 2-1 **Key Themes in the Geezer Interviews**

GEEZERS

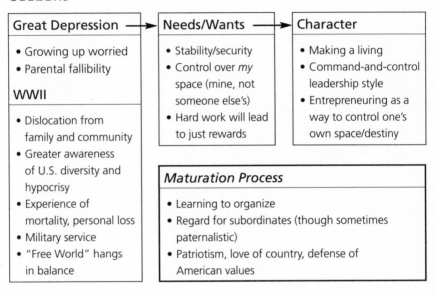

Great Depression	Needs/Wants	Character
• Growing up worried • Parental fallibility **WWII** • Dislocation from family and community • Greater awareness of U.S. diversity and hypocrisy • Experience of mortality, personal loss • Military service • "Free World" hangs in balance	• Stability/security • Control over *my* space (mine, not someone else's) • Hard work will lead to just rewards	• Making a living • Command-and-control leadership style • Entrepreneuring as a way to control one's own space/destiny

Maturation Process

- Learning to organize
- Regard for subordinates (though sometimes paternalistic)
- Patriotism, love of country, defense of American values

In what we've identified as the Era of Limits, geezers were living the Game of Life. Like the game, life contained elements of chance. You couldn't predict how far you might go in a career or how successful your marriage and family life might turn out to be. But the prospect of a conventional career and a conventional family was largely taken for granted. You could anticipate one career trajectory—in one field with one or perhaps two companies—much as there was only one path to success in the board game. The rules for success were pretty clear: work hard, produce results, and you'll get promoted and receive a pension (presumably supplemented by Social Security) to underwrite your retirement. Provide for your family and set a good example for your kids, and you'll complete the game happily. Sloan Wilson's 1956 portrayal of the white-collar world in *The Man in the Gray Flannel Suit* mirrored Alfred P. Sloan's definition of the modern business executive: "Master and servant of the large-scale corporation."

The notion of "one life" (or one chance at the game) that dominated geezers' thinking at age 25–30 was directly influenced by their own experiences as well as those of their parents in the wake of the Great Depression, and by their own search for stability following the upheaval of World War II.[11] As children of the Depression, most of them grew up worried. They knew their parents were fallible because they had seen them broken by the loss of homes and jobs. As a result, they began adulthood seeking a certain financial security above all else. An apt case in point is Sidney Harman, now 82 and the chairman of the board of the multibillion-dollar audio equipment manufacturer Harman International. In his teens, Harman equated success in life with a steady paycheck: "If someone came along with a lifetime contract to pay me five thousand dollars a year, that would be success. When I was thirty, it was making money. Success then was running the . . . business and running it well and being recognized for the fact that I was doing it and getting paid. That was success."

Mike Wallace, 82, of CBS News and co-creator of the path-breaking program *60 Minutes*, defined success at age 21 as:

> *Ten thousand bucks a year. And a certain security. Look, I came from immigrant parents. Both of them came from Russia—my Dad at sixteen, my mother when she was a year and a half, and who were devotees of Franklin Roosevelt. To them he was hope and promise and opportunity. And growing up in those Depression years was a very, very tough time. I worked, you know. I either washed dishes or waited on table at various fraternity houses around the campus. And didn't get much money from home. Had a National Youth Administration job that paid thirty dollars a month or something like that.*

Like Wallace, geezers often use their family of origin as the backdrop against which to locate their aspirations and—without a trace of smugness—to compare their accomplishments. Dee

Hock, 71-year-old CEO emeritus of Visa International, recounted his upbringing:

> *I am the sixth of six children. Born in a little tiny mountain community in Utah. My parents had an eighth-grade education. We lived in a two-room house. No plumbing, no running water. Maybe had six to seven hundred square feet in it. And it was kind of in the country, farming community at the base of the Wasatch Range of the Rockies. . . . My wife's the eleventh of twelve children, raised in a little hardscrabble farm, same thing. Father died of cancer in high school. Straight-A student but couldn't go to college until she was middle-aged.*

In other words, these young people valued what their parents had provided them, but they were also determined to do better for their own children.

Warren Bennis identified the day his father came home jobless as an inflection point in his life:

> *When I was about five or six, my father lost his job. And he was totally helpless. He had no recourse. There was no Social Security. There was no pension. And for the next few years it was a real struggle. I mean, he did jobs like loading booze, illicit booze on trucks. He ran summonses for lawyers. He distributed flyers for the Republican Party to earn a buck, or earn a quarter I mean, not a buck. And when he came home and told my mother he'd lost his job, she broke into tears and I felt, 'I'm never going to let that happen to me. I'm never going to be at the effect of other people who are going to be able to do that to me. I'm not going to be in a position where I will ever, ever, allow myself to be vulnerable to that helplessness.'*

Military Imprint

Service in the military, particularly during World War II, left its mark on both the aspirations and the skills geezers took with them into the Era of Limits. Howe and Strauss, in their pioneering work on generational differences in America, summarized it nicely: "Returning war heroes brought a mature, no-nonsense attitude wherever they went—to campuses, to workplaces, to politics."[12] John Gardner, founder of Common Cause and cofounder of the Independent Sector and a professor at Stanford University when he died in 2002 at age 89, talked about the profound effect his stint as a Marine officer had on his self-concept:

> *I was a very reserved, aloof young man. I was an observer . . . I didn't think of myself as in the mix of things. And I had to come out of that. And the Marine Corps helped me a lot. Just simple fundamentals of leadership. If you're not acting like a leader with Marine Corps enlisted men, they let you know. And they brought me out.*

Ed Guthman, an aide to Attorney General Robert F. Kennedy before becoming a Pulitzer Prize–winning journalist and newspaper editor, recalled the way military service shaped the behavior of the Kennedy administration in the early 1960s:

> *[O]ne of the things about the Kennedy administration which was unique in a sense, almost everybody had been in combat. They had been noncoms, junior officers, and enlisted men. And the president had been. I mean it wasn't just flying over in an airplane. It was really in there. And I think that had a real effect on that administration . . . in an organizing sense. We had that ability to do things rather quickly. And I think it was our military experience that made the difference.*

Getting Ahead

Hard work, dedication, ambition, and native ability/intelligence explained who "got ahead" and who didn't, at least in the eyes of the geezers we interviewed. Indeed, the very term "career" was synonymous with salary and rank. Bill Porter, 74-year-old founder of E*Trade, took a job at General Electric not long after mustering out of the Navy and, while at GE, found his marker in the system of promotion and compensation: "I think probably the most important thing in those days was promotion within GE. I think that was, you know, climbing up through the empire. I don't know if that's power. . . . Big money, yes."

Don Gevirtz, 71, founder of the Foothill Group and, later, U.S. ambassador to Fiji, depicted success at age 30 in simple terms: "[I]n those days . . . all most of us could think of was to make money and get rich. And accumulate enough money so that would be a marker. I'm embarrassed to tell you that now, but that's what kept driving me."

Though later to become the first woman to own a seat on the New York Stock Exchange, in her twenties Muriel Siebert calibrated success in terms of the kind of vacation she took and whether or not she could afford a new car.

Work was central to geezers' social identity at age 25–30. They thought a lot about "becoming somebody," leaving a distinct impression that identity was something you grew into. And for many, identity derived from organizational affiliation. Many of the geezers had been intensely loyal to corporations, at least until they left to create their own businesses. A secure job with a generous company was sweet to people who remembered all too clearly what unemployment felt like.

True, the companies they flocked to often had now-unfashionable bureaucratic administrations and dress codes that required uniforms of gray-flannel suits and subdued ties. As Bill Porter reminded us, big companies were often the targets of criticism from young careerists:

> *A friend and I used to go duck hunting in upstate New York and we'd sit in these duck blinds and there would never be any ducks, but we used to sit there and cuss out the GE management. OK? About everything they were doing wrong and how staid they were and they wouldn't make changes and so forth and so on.*

*And maybe a little bit we were right, but I think probably the
most important thing in those days was promotion within GE.*

And, as Muriel Siebert pointed out, Wall Street and most of big
business was "not nice" to women (or to Jews, as she describes in
the sidebar that follows) who aspired to a career:

*I was a partner of a small firm, Finkel and Company, because I
could not get hired by a large firm and get credit on the business.
They did not have women. We just were not there. They had
women as secretaries; sometimes they had an analyst or two; but
we were secretaries. This was a period of time that was not nice
on Wall Street. I remember, I wanted to change jobs because the
men were being paid twice what I was being paid. And I had
changed jobs twice. And I sent out a resume with my name on it
to every firm downtown and did not get one interview. The
NYSSA sent the same resume out with my initials on it, and that's
how I got to Shields. And I got an interview and a job. So that
was the real world.*

Stinging though these assessments are, both Porter and Siebert
ultimately affirmed rather than indicted the system. Indeed, the
blanket condemnation of the Organization Man in recent years
obscures an important facet of the Era of Limits. These same corporations enabled an entire generation to buy homes in the suburbs, educate their children, and develop management and even
leadership skills that would serve them well for decades to come.
As a result, most of our older leaders have had one, two, or, at
most, three careers in the course of fifty years.

Paying Your Dues

Geezers treat experience as a symbol of achievement and as a sign of
commitment. For instance, Mike Wallace told us of a frustrating

M URIEL SIEBERT talked about a triple-whammy that dogged her early days on Wall Street: being female, Jewish, and not a lawyer. In this instance, she described her own way of addressing anti-Semitism:

I had seen anti-Semitism downtown when I was selling stocks because at times I would go out with people and they worked for major institutions and at that time, it was extremely common to have a drink at lunch. I mean, that was part of doing business. You'd have a drink or two at lunch. And give somebody a couple of drinks and they would talk about the Jews. And I had a greeting card that I used for those occasions. It went like this:

> *Roses are reddish*
> *Violets are bluish*
> *In case you don't know*
> *I am Jewish.*

I had that card delivered to them by hand, and I said, 'Enjoyed lunch, Mickie.' They got that card in the afternoon, and I never had to take any of that nonsense again. And I never embarrassed anyone, either.

conversation he'd recently had with a young woman less than a third his age. Opening his hands plaintively, he said: "I told her, 'You have not done enough about paying your dues.' And I believe this. I really do. I mean, she's a really wonderful young woman. But you've got to start here and then learn and then move up a little bit. And learn some more. But she's here and there and what. I mean, she's like a lightning bug!"

For geezers, "paying your dues" indicated two very important things: that you were prepared to endure an event or master a body of knowledge *and* that you were willing to demonstrate respect for those who did the same before you. Sometimes frustration with younger people was palpable among our geezers (see the following sidebar). And, for many geezers a major component of success in the early years of their careers was simple recognition for "a job well done." The sentiment was strongly held among the men and women whose parents held working-class, farming, and technical jobs—the "thinker-doers" as described by David Halberstam.[13]

BILL PORTER, founder of E*Trade and holder of numerous patents from his days at General Electric, expressed some common geezer sentiments about "paying your dues." He spoke in the fall of 2000 with some despair about the young people pursuing their fortunes via e-commerce:

The kids of today just expect it to be handed to them. And the worst case in that sense, even though they are motivated to do things, the young folks that are starting these e-commerce organizations, they just expect the money to come rolling in. What is it? Over half of the high school students think they're going to be millionaires? Well, that just isn't so. And they've got to get out and work and they'll learn, I guess. But life has come to them so easily that I guess the leaders will come forth. And I don't see the world coming to no good end or anything of that sort. But I certainly don't see the work ethic and so forth that at least my generation had.

In a later conversation, following the precipitous fall of e-commerce stocks in 2001, Porter was bit more optimistic: "The young people who come out of this with their heads held high and anxious to try again are the ones I'd say you should hire. They'll have failed big, sure. But if they have the will to come back, then they're the ones to snatch up."

During the interviews, for example, 71-year-old judge Nathaniel Jones, whose father had been a steelworker and his mother a domestic, and 91-year-old coach John Wooden, whose father had been a farmer and school teacher, both underscored the great sense of self-satisfaction they received from recognition of a job well done, even as young children. John Brademas, 72-year-old president emeritus of New York University and former congressional leader, recalled his father repeating to him a phrase in ancient Greek: "My father used to say, 'Here are the words of Socrates [in Greek]: "Things of value come only after hard work.' " And he would add, 'John, if that's all the Greek you ever learn, that's all you need to know.' "

In addition to conveying tangibility and immediacy to the idea of success, this focus on the task bespoke an air of legitimacy to organizational hierarchy. For example, 78-year-old Elizabeth McCormack described success in her first few years in the Order of the Sacred Heart in the following way: "You did what you were told to do. Whether it was teach a class, work with children, be the headmistress of a school. . . . You could say you were successful when the person who was your superior and who you believed was the voice of God for you, when that person felt you were doing an OK job or a very good job. That was success."

Ed Guthman, the 76-year old journalist and newspaper editor, recalled at age 25 unquestioningly trusting the judgment of his senior editors. Russell McGrath, his editor at the *Seattle Times*, told him to rewrite a story about a University of Washington professor who'd been labeled a communist by a state-level un-American affairs committee. Get more depth and detail, Guthman was told. Without question, Guthman followed orders: "I think it was my military training," he said. "He was my commander and I followed his orders." Guthman's reporting won a Pulitzer Prize for the story.

To judge a job well done, however, organizational superiors had to know at least as much about the work as the person doing it—if not more. In the 1950s, managers were expected to be accomplished, if not expert, in the fields they supervised. Thus, far from being an idle compliment or an item ticked on an annual performance evaluation, the judgment of a superior, a veteran, an elder, had meaning. Age and experience counted.

Learning in Traditional Ways

For geezers at age 25–30, important things came to those who learned the ropes, heeded their elders, played according to the rules, and demonstrated patience. Higher education is an institution esteemed by most of our senior leaders, especially those who saw that college and graduate school offered them opportunities—intellectual, social, and professional—that other members of their families never had. A taste for learning, especially for books as a window on other worlds, came directly from their families. Sidney Rittenberg, 78-year-old consultant to businesses and governments dealing with China, recalled the soothing sound of his sisters reading poetry to him as a sickly child. Coach John Wooden attributed his love of language to his father's nightly recitations of poetry in their Indiana farmhouse. And John Brademas, former majority whip in the U.S. House of Representatives, opened his arms wide to depict a child's memory of the expansiveness of his grandfather's library: "In this little town of Swayzee—population seven hundred—my grandfather, a retired history professor, had a library of seven thousand books. I practically lived in that library. And that exposed me at an early age to books that I might not have come across even in school."

Frances Hesselbein's eyes sparkled when she recalled her grandmother's role in her early education:

She used to read poetry to me and read stories. And she remembered all the family stories, so she could talk about the Civil War as though it were yesterday. And she went to a one-room schoolhouse, way back in the mountains where her family had a lumber mill that made barrel staves since the 1840s. So she went to a one-room schoolhouse where her father and grandfather had gone to school. And above the blackboard, and it could have

*come from McGuffy, fifty years earlier, there was . . . she made
me memorize this: "If wisdom's ways you would wisely seek,
these five things observe with care: Of whom you speak, to
whom you speak, how, when, and where." And the only time
I've ever gotten into trouble in my life was when I forgot that.
You see, you always think "of whom you speak, to whom you
speak, how, when and where." Now that is early frontier wisdom. Great leadership advice.*

Geezers were (and are) avid readers, and their bookshelves are
packed with classic works of fiction and nonfiction—the stuff of
which Western civilization and great books curricula were made.
Geezers ask, "What have you read recently?" When we asked
their favorite works of fiction, we got the following list:

- *The Emigrants,* by W. G. Sebald
- *Diary of a Seducer,* by Søren Kierkegaard
- *On the Black Hill,* by Bruce Chatwin
- Novels of Graham Greene and Evelyn Waugh
- All the works of Shakespeare
- *Woman in White,* by Wilkie Collins
- *Memoirs of a Geisha,* by Arthur Golden
- *Huckleberry Finn,* by Mark Twain
- *The Invisible Man,* by Ralph Ellison
- Novels by Charles Dickens
- *Anna Karenina,* by Leo Tolstoy
- *War and Peace,* by Leo Tolstoy
- *The End of the Affair,* by Graham Greene
- *The Grapes of Wrath,* by John Steinbeck
- *Holy Bible*
- *Angela's Ashes,* by Frank McCourt

Perhaps because older leaders were schooled in canonical
works, like those of Shakespeare, Tolstoy, and Dickens, some

lamented what they perceived to be a shallowness in contemporary approaches to learning. Paolo Soleri, 82-year-old architect, ceramicist, and urban planner, wondered about the effect the Internet has had on how children learn:

The enlarging of the potential that, for instance, the Internet brings in is matched by maybe a shallowness that is very much generated by the speed by which things are happening. So for instance in my development, I was sluggish and very, very elementary and very few things were happening compared to what's going on now for a young person. But maybe that had the virtue of letting me sit on my ego and eventually get more knowledgeable. Because I think now we are in love with data and information and we are missing the acknowledgment that comes from a slow process of learning, a slow process of growing and so on.

To say that geezers grew up in an Era of Limits is not to imply that they accepted their situation cheerfully and without question. Indeed, many felt, as writer Dorothy Parker put it, "trapped like a trap in a trap." But even the geezers who broke free—like Jack Coleman who by the age of 75 had been a college president, a banker, a foundation president, a garbage collector, a New York City cop, and a homeless vagrant—drew comfort and a feeling of safe harbor from the pursuit of well-defined work, family, and social roles.

Career and Family

Despite the attention the topic has received in recent years—not least from Secretary of Labor Elaine Chao[14]—balancing career and family was not a high-visibility issue in the Era of Limits. If anything, it was a private matter to be worked out in kitchens and bedrooms, not in the press or in legislative hearings. Whereas 90 percent of the mothers of the young leaders we interviewed worked outside the home (see table 2-2), nearly 90 percent of

Table 2-2 Comparative Features of Geezer and Geek
           Interviewees

	Geezers	Geeks
Age range	70–93	21–34
Average age	77	28
Birth year (based on average age)	1924	1973
When 25–30	1945–1951	1991–2003
Gender (male/female)	88%/22%	61%/39%
% with divorced parents	8%	44%
Average number of siblings	2.4	1.8
Father's occupation		
Executive/managerial	32%	6%
Professional/technical	16%	44%
Entrepreneur/small business	20%	11%
Farmer	12%	0%
Service (white-collar)	0%	39%
Manufacturing (blue-collar)	20%	0%
Mother's occupation		
Executive/managerial	0%	0%
Professional/technical	0%	14%
Entrepreneur/small business	0%	21%
Farmer	0%	0%
Service (white-collar)	13%	57%
Manufacturing (blue-collar)	0%	0%
Worked at home	87%	7%
% married between age 21 and 30	80%	50%
% ever married	92%	50%
% with children	92%	39%
Average age of children	45	4
Average age at birth of first child	27	28

geezers' mothers were housewives. Thus, only a small fraction of geezers had even a passing familiarity with two-career families. What they and their parents knew was the two-person career: He toiled for a salary and she did the things that made it possible for him to move up the ladder.

Consider what Robert Crandall, retired chairman of the board of American Airlines, had to say on the topic:

> *For all the years that I was working, I was trying to achieve a particular goal. So I wasn't interested in balance. I didn't sail very much. I didn't play any golf. I didn't take much time off. I ran American Airlines and it pretty much took up my whole life. Which suited me fine. I was having a great time. . . . Now you read a lot about balance. In today's world people say, "I have to have a more balanced life. I have to have time for my kids and my job and my hobbies." That's all well and good. But people who worry about balance have no overriding passion to achieve leadership.*

Most geezers, like Crandall, grew up believing that a traditional marital division of labor was already balanced. His ability to function as an executive (or, more broadly, as a leader and public figure) assumed the existence of someone else to organize and support his career. For example, Ned Regan, 70-year-old former controller for the state of New York and now president of Baruch College, saw imbalance as an unavoidable feature of having a professional career—in his case, politics: "When you're in public life and you're out four nights a week, something gives. And that's it. And so that was not exactly a strong part of what I did. It was just [that] public life and a complete strong family life [were] kind of inconsistent if you really wanted to continue to do your job, if you wanted to continue to be with people and go to the big dinners and do what you have to do."

Looking backward in time, some geezers wished they had addressed the issue of balance more at an earlier point in their lives, though not necessarily at age 25–30. Several spoke movingly about the moments in their children's lives they'd missed while fixated on getting ahead. For example, Jack Coleman, former president of Haverford College, MIT professor, and chair of the Federal Reserve Bank of Philadelphia, offered this poignant reflection: "One of the greatest sorrows I will carry to my dying day is that I never saw my youngest son on the stage and he was at a private school, the Westown School. I don't think it's twenty minutes away from the Haverford campus. I never saw him. I was too busy. And I'm going to regret that forever."

Coleman was also painfully honest when he noted that failing to achieve balance in another facet of his life—a failed marriage—enabled him to do things he might not otherwise have been able to: "The truth is I've been able to do things I wouldn't have been able to do if I were married. I wouldn't have the freedom to go where my heart and head say to go without having to ask my partner, 'Is it OK if I let my heart and my head tell me go this way and leave you at this time and go away and disappear for a while?' What enormous freedom I've had to just pick up and go."

Frances Hesselbein, now CEO of the Drucker Foundation, in the 1950s enacted a role far more typical for women of her generation: She was first and foremost a wife, mother, and community volunteer. Before going on to head the world's largest women's organization, the Girl Scouts, Hesselbein defined success this way: "[Success was] having my son grow up to be a healthy, happy person, and helping my husband in his work and doing the kind of work in the community that made a difference. I really saw it in the widest possible perspective. But at thirty . . . I felt as old as I would ever feel. At thirty I was just terribly grown up and sophisticated and didn't realize how dumb I really was at that age."

For most geezers, balance was something you achieved over the span of your life. That is, you focused less attention on family and self in the younger and middle stages of your career and more later (particularly following formal retirement). For most women, however, the order was reversed: Career was something you might take up once traditional motherhood responsibilities had been fulfilled.

An Era of Heroic Leaders

Geezers at age 25–30 were profoundly influenced by the larger-than-life heroes of their times. In interviews they mentioned:

- Franklin D. Roosevelt
- Ghandi
- Abraham Lincoln
- Nelson Mandela
- John F. Kennedy
- Winston Churchill
- Alan Greenspan
- Eleanor Roosevelt
- Jean Pierre Trudeau
- Harry Truman
- Martin Luther King, Jr.
- Nelson Rockefeller
- Jimmy Carter
- Adlai Stevenson
- Lao Tzu
- Henry David Thoreau
- Howard Baker
- Beethoven
- Mother Theresa

Our geezers came of age in an era of embattled and challenged institutions. Great leaders were needed and, thankfully, great leaders emerged. The very idea of heroic leadership was deeply entrenched in public discourse, as well as in the education of schoolchildren, during the war and its aftermath. Heroes and villains alike were portrayed in exaggerated, cartoon-like imagery, and the conflicts between nations and ideologies took the form of battles between oversized icons. Heroes could become politicians and politicians could become heroes.

Is it any wonder, then, that military concepts like unit cohesion, chain of command, and discipline were widely accepted by the public at large and our geezers in particular because they had proven their worth in World War II? Supervisors were to be regarded like officers in the military: You obeyed them because you learned you had to as part of military discipline and because you hoped they had your best interests in mind. Dee Hock, accomplished businessman turned educator and philosopher, recalled with relish his days as a "command-and-control alcoholic": "I often tell people that I am really a command-and-control alcoholic. I know how to do that! . . . If you get twelve corporate CEOs up to the bar and open a case of command and control, I'll drink them all under the table!"

This is not to say that all geezers embraced command and control. And some, like Hock, did so early on but later changed their style. However, in the context of the Era of Limits, where military training, large-scale industry, and a deep-seated belief in the notion of "bigger is better" prevailed, the safest option in selecting a leadership style was what Douglas McGregor would later call "Theory X."[15]

———

In the aftermath of the Great Depression and World War II, geezers hungered for a good job, a healthy family, and a home free from disruption. Rolling up their sleeves, they went to college and back to work, engendering the Baby Boom, urban exodus, highway culture, and the spread of the American Dream. The Era of Limits was a time of cautious optimism—a period in which men and women alike were encouraged to play the game hard but to play it by the rules, to be loyal to company and country with the expectation that such loyalty would be rewarded. Leaders grew up with plenty of icons to emulate, but it was the experience of war and the discipline of industry that favored a self-reliant Lone Ranger kind of leader. And, of course, the Era of Limits was a time of rigid gender and family roles that yielded few opportunities for men and women to lead in the same sphere.

Now let's look at the geeks, who came of age between 1991 and 2000—the Era of Options: a high-speed, media-saturated age offering limitless choice, but no clear direction.

THREE

Geeks

The Era of Options

GODFREY WARNER, a fictional (but familiar) geezer CEO, recently hired a talented, 30-year-old M.B.A. into his manufacturing firm. At the interview, Warner could see the kid was brimming with ideas and energy, a born leader. But within a few short months, the relationship soured. The new employee seemed restless; he left the office early, and Warner suspected that he might even be using work time to cultivate other career contacts online. Inevitably, the new hire tucked his laptop under his arm and breezed on to the next job. Asked what went wrong, a frustrated Warner threw up his hands, "I don't know," he sighed, "I can't figure these kids out."

That story played itself out thousands of times during the height of the Internet-frenzy of the mid- to late-1990s. Senior executives, many of them geezers or near-geezers, scratched their heads in wonderment as they watched critical talent and future

leaders stream out the front door of marbled corporate headquar-
ters in order to take up residency in a one-room "bull pen" of an
e-commerce start-up. Most CEOs of big companies already had
their immediate successors chosen and waiting (however impa-
tiently) in the wings; what they feared, however, was the out-
migration of the generation of leaders after their successors.
Where would they come from? Would they be interested in a corporate career when they could grow their own business instead?
We call this period—from 1991 to 2000—the Era of Options.

The Era of Options: 1991–2000

In the absence of conflict on a global scale, this was a time of small,
made-for-television wars with snappy titles like "Desert Storm."
Few young Americans saw actual combat, but images of mass
graves filled with civilian bones in Bosnia and Somalia haunted
the nightly news. The world was riven by dozens of ethnic and
territorial battles occurring simultaneously. A United Nations
study in 1999 provided a snapshot of the "New World Order":
twenty-five armed border disputes involving forty nations in a
single year. Some disputes, like those in the Middle East and in
Ireland, would seem resolved only to flare up again dramatically.

The idea of "police action" was new when President Truman
used it in 1950 to describe his muddled involvement in Korea, but
both the term and the policy it describes survived through the end
of the twentieth century in Somalia, Haiti, and Bosnia. For a
global superpower that consistently reacted to conflicts as a sort
of "police," many believed that the concept of a national foreign
policy may have become defunct.

The world stage was chaotic and volatile. The demise of the
Soviet Union set off a dangerous chain reaction of "descending"
states, like Russia, and "ascending" states, like China. Caught in the
lurch of these massive power shifts were "messy" states, disorgan-
ized nations with corrupt governments, like Somalia and the former
Yugoslavia. Finally, the ever-present threat of terrorism at home
and abroad exposed American vulnerability, superpower or not.

Politics Becomes Entertainment

Media-savvy young people increasingly saw themselves as a "target market," consumers of political platforms as much as sports drinks or Gameboys. Themes from the sixties like TV, rock music, contraceptive use, and the openness of violence and sex gave way to new variations: PBS was muscled aside by MTV; the freedom of the Pill yielded to the safety of the condom; the physicality of Vietnam, Kent State, and Free Love succumbed to the vicarious thrills of Hollywood-manufactured violence and sex. And thanks to the proliferation of wireless phones and e-mail, communication also became ubiquitous.

Nearly twenty years after the Watergate break-in, Americans remained skeptical about political institutions. They voted in smaller and smaller percentages, and a plague of political apathy spread across college campuses. Boundaries between politics and entertainment blurred as MTV urged this generation to "Rock the Vote," and a presidential hopeful appeared on television wearing dark shades and playing a saxophone. Polls, popularity ratings, and lobbyist dollars determined government policy. Little wonder that American youth maintained an ironic distance from the process.

Yet the political process hobbled on, largely unchallenged by American voters despite debacles like the government shutdown over unresolved congressional partisanship, President Clinton's impeachment, and the badly mangled presidential election of 2000. They gave one sitting president abysmal ratings on his personal integrity, and they scoffed at the intelligence of another—but still they did not abandon the political system.

Fast-Forward Economy

Despite some internal upheaval, big business was as potent as ever. Extraordinary advances in computing and communication technologies incited a dramatic shuffling in big business ranks. Moore's Law scripted a fundamental rewriting of information processing, and the growing World Wide Web launched telecommunications.[1]

These two developments signaled the arrival of new markets, new competitors, and new forms of organizing.

Even with retrenchment among Internet start-ups and a new-found respect for profitability among venture capitalists, this was an era frothing with experimentation: for example, flat and flexible networked organizations, team-based production, stock options instead of salary, and e-commerce exchanges. The 1950s model of the Organization Man seemed targeted for extinction from all sides. He was replaced by an amazing, and probably unstable, mix of alternatives: e-lancers, temporary workers, contingent and contract workers, professionals-for-hire, wannabe and soon-to-be entrepreneurs. As companies honed operating costs to a minimum and reacted to what seemed like an endless parade of changes in markets and technologies, the idea of reciprocal loyalty between organization and employee went out the window. Companies like Apple Computer offered a chance to learn and to have fun for a time, but they didn't offer careers.[2] Young employees learned not to expect traditional careers; they anticipated, even craved, nine or more different employers by the time they reached middle age.

Among the most important developments was the relentless acceleration in the pace of business. At the conclusion of a panel held in 2000, the founder of an acclaimed Internet start-up was asked what he thought he might teach the veteran CEO he'd hired to head up the rapidly growing company. With a grin, he replied, "Speed." Certainly speed became a watchword for Internet-based companies, particularly in key business processes like Web site design and deployment, customer service, order fulfillment, and product development. When competitors could quickly copy (or trump) your last move, you had to go fast faster.

Images and icons of leadership in this era tended to revolve around a different axis than in the fifties. The "all-purpose heroes" celebrated by *Time* magazine no longer existed. When we asked explicitly for heroes and leadership icons, teenagers and others under 30 were likely to cite their parents or to claim that they find the hero concept irrelevant—a dramatic shift from the 1950s. Command and control did not recede entirely, but older business leaders like Jack Welch, Arie de Geus, and Dee Hock talked much more often about participation, engagement, and collaboration as the central leadership mechanisms.

Smothered in Possibilities

Much like the early 1950s, this era boasted enormous economic growth unevenly distributed among the population. But unlike the fifties, young men and women in the nineties were "smothered in possibilities." While kids who grew up in the fifties may have felt the claustrophobia of their limited choices, kids of this era felt the agoraphobia of seemingly unlimited opportunity.

Newspapers in the early nineties were filled with tales of college students who scrawled a business plan on a pizza box, won a dizzying amount of venture capital, and launched an Internet-based business during their junior year. The youth culture was categorized and analyzed in the media as never before: They were Baby Busters, Slackers, Thirteeners (for the thirteenth generation), Twenty-nothings, Dot-comers, Gen X, and Gen Y. Minority groups exercised a clear influence on cultural norms (hip-hop music and fashion and the diversity movements in academia and corporate America are prime examples), no doubt a result of the increases in the minority population. According to census data, when geezers grew up, roughly 15 percent of the population under 18 was non-white versus closer to 33 percent for the era during which geeks grew up.

Gen X and Gen Y emerged as the dominant generational labels, distinguishing between kids born in the 1970s and those born in the mid-1980s onward. The distinction had as much to do with the circumstances they were born into as the attitudes they (purportedly) displayed. The idea that Gen Xers were "slackers" was popularized by a 1991 movie of the same name, and was reinforced by the popularity of "grunge" music. This group, the story went, graduated from college during an economic downturn that offered only McJobs with no future. They hung out in coffeehouses wearing battered flannel shirts and sneering at the corporate culture and middle-class values of the boomers. They grew up during the late 1980s wave of reengineering and downsizing that left their parents pink-slipped from companies that once seemed to promise lifelong employment. Their childhood coincided with the years that an article in the *Atlantic Monthly* magazine calls "the most virulently anti-child period in American history," the age of the "latchkey child," "throwaway child," and "boomerang child."[3]

Gen Y, by contrast, is a generation that has known only economic prosperity. Higher salaries and more flexible work arrangements turned many of their parents into "soccer moms" and "take your kid to work" dads. As the zeitgeist became more child-centered, members of Gen Y started building killer resumes as adolescents. Yet the age difference between Gen X and Gen Y is only five to ten years, a separation of two siblings, not a whole generation. Consequently, the frictions that arose between the two "generations" felt like a sibling rivalry: Family circumstances had improved since the birth of the first child, and the later child grew up amidst greater prosperity. As one Gen X writer complained, "Already [our] straighter siblings are stealing the spotlight. . . . It's enough to make me want to score a Beemer and start working on a cell phone tumor."[4]

On the family front, American women of all ages flocked into the labor market, often following in the footsteps of their boomer mothers. While some women worked out of necessity to bolster sagging working- and middle-class family incomes, many worked for the same reason Eleanor Roosevelt cited back in the fifties—self-fulfillment. Achieving economic parity with men also became a goal of many career women. Ultimately, two-paycheck and two-career households displaced the fifties version of the nuclear family with a breadwinner dad and a stay-at-home mom.

Dramatic increases in the rate of divorce and in single parenting (often aided by advances in reproductive technology) led to a remarkably diverse array of family forms. "Family values" eclipsed the rest of the political platform for both parties, but fifties nostalgia clashed with demographic reality. Politicians tried to reconcile a yearning for the stability of the nuclear family with the needs of single mothers, gay and lesbian parents, intergenerational families, and families struggling to adjust to welfare reform. Census figures reported that the nuclear family had dropped to around 25 percent of all family forms, and the percentage of households with children under the age of 18 slipped to 23.5 percent in 2000, in comparison to 45 percent in 1960.[5]

As American education reached a crisis point and test scores plummeted, public schools, once the pride of the suburbs and a hallmark of American democracy, lost popular support. In cities and towns throughout the nation, families with adequate resources redirected their children to private schools. Parochial schools grew popular as an alternative to public schools in which parents had no confidence or elite private schools that they could not afford.

Organized religion receded in importance in this era, while spiritualism, New Age philosophy, and holistic living gained popularity. Fewer people were filling the pews of traditional churches and synagogues and more were investigating Eastern traditions like Zen Buddhism. Rather than patronize an institution, many geeks practiced yoga and meditation from their homes. They were also, as *Fortune* pointed out, more "willing to talk about bringing their faith to work. . . . However, they speak of 'spirituality' and 'meaning,' not 'religion' and 'God.' "[6] They sought this meaning in "awareness-raising" activities like wearing pins in support of breast cancer research, participating in the Walk for Hunger, or attending charitable rock concerts such as Farm Aid, Amnesty International, or Free Tibet.

Geeks at Age 25–30

What were the men and women we interviewed under the age of 35 thinking about in the period of 1991–2000? What impact did the Era of Options have on them as individuals and as leaders? Figure 3-1 summarizes key themes that emerged from the interviews with our under-35 leaders. It also highlights the causal relations that people drew as they explained the effect of era on their own lives.

Figure 3-1 **Key Themes in the Geek Interviews**

GEEKS

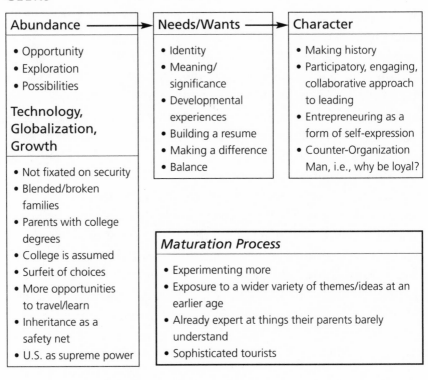

Abundance ────►	Needs/Wants ────►	Character
• Opportunity • Exploration • Possibilities **Technology, Globalization, Growth** • Not fixated on security • Blended/broken families • Parents with college degrees • College is assumed • Surfeit of choices • More opportunities to travel/learn • Inheritance as a safety net • U.S. as supreme power	• Identity • Meaning/ significance • Developmental experiences • Building a resume • Making a difference • Balance	• Making history • Participatory, engaging, collaborative approach to leading • Entrepreneuring as a form of self-expression • Counter-Organization Man, i.e., why be loyal?

Maturation Process
• Experimenting more • Exposure to a wider variety of themes/ideas at an earlier age • Already expert at things their parents barely understand • Sophisticated tourists

Making History

Geeks, we found, harbor grander and more ambitious aspirations than geezers did at the same age, and they are impatient to achieve them. To get a handle on this generational difference, compare the earlier declaration from Sidney Harman ("If someone came along with a lifetime contract to pay me five thousand dollars a year, that would be success") with what we heard from ardent young leaders like Harlan Hugh, 24-year-old CTO and cofounder of The Brain Technologies Corporation, a knowledge management software company. Hugh began programming computers at age 6 and matter-of-factly concluded: "I always knew that I wanted to start a software company. And I always knew that I wanted to try and change the world, really. That was always part of my thinking and . . . part of the culture that was inside of my household."

Listen also to Wendy Kopp, the 32-year-old founder of the highly praised Teach For America program: "I really wanted to do something that would make an impact on the world. I know this sounds crazy, but even as a student I kept telling myself, 'I'm just gaining the skills to be able to apply this towards something that really matters, that really will make the world a better place.' "

We heard something quite similar from Lingyun Shao, chosen by *Glamour* magazine in 2000 as one of the ten young women to watch. Shao, a sergeant in the U.S. Army Reserve, a trained nurse, and a student of nuclear engineering by the age of 23, recognized that her accomplishments had earned her the sobriquet from *Glamour*. However, when she met the other nine award-winners, she realized that she shared ambitions in common with many more people her age:

> *At first I thought, "These are gonna be a resume-pushing people." But we got on really well, because it turns out that all ten of us are trying to find this like altered reality, or this utopia, or we're trying to change the world and make it into this world we want it to be. And it was inspiring to meet people who thought, who also thought that they could really make a difference, you know, despite what everyone else tells you.*

Contrary to the bad press generated by conspicuous consumption among a few Internet entrepreneurs, the geeks we interviewed described a strong sense of obligation to the communities that surround them. We did not find the 1990s version of Gordon Gekko, the greedy and relentless corporate raider (played with slicked-back hair by Michael Douglas in Oliver Stone's 1987 film, *Wall Street*). Personal wealth carries real social obligations. For example, Lingyun Shao talked about achieving personal financial security in the business sector and then building a medical practice that embodied her personal philosophy of providing quality medical care to indigenous communities. Others, like Young Shin,

30-year-old cofounder of Internet start-up Embark.com, anticipated becoming educators, perhaps even high school teachers,
once their businesses stabilized. Shin told us, for example:

> I think the most impact you can have on society and people and
> the world in general is to be incredibly successful with this busi-
> ness, with my next business, with being advisor to other compa-
> nies and so on. . . . At some point five or ten years down the line,
> if I am wealthy and successful, I can then turn that into an advi-
> sory role and as a philanthropist and those other things. Give
> back to the community and give it back in a bigger way than just
> writing checks as an example.

Others, like Brian Morris, an African-American financial advisor, saw their task as not just philanthropy or momentary infusions
of energy and attention but as one of making a sustainable difference in a part of society that mattered to them. Describing his
own strategy for giving back to his community, Morris told us: "I
recognized that someone had to create an entity and our community—and when I say our community, African-American community—that was of us and from us. When Charles Merrill started
Merrill Lynch back in the late 1800s, or whatever year it was, he
was hell-bent on creating something that had perpetuity. I wanted
to do the same thing."

Statements like "change the world" and "make the world a
better place" might sound like enthusiastic declarations of youth
in any era, but when you look at their accomplishments you come
away impressed by the things they've already done at an early
age. Before the age of 30, fourteen out of eighteen geeks had
started a multimillion dollar company. Over a third had received
national recognition for their achievements. Three had built
organizations that were emulated across the nation.

Making Wealth

Aspirations to "change the world" have their material coun-
terpart in "making wealth." Indeed, it was Jeff Wilke, 33-year-

old senior vice president at Amazon.com, who first alerted us to these twin ambitions as he explained his decision to leave an executive position at a more traditional manufacturing firm: "I wanted to make personal wealth and I wanted to make history." Similarly, early on in his work life, 29-year-old Internet company CEO Michael Klein made a priority of achieving personal wealth: "I had about twenty million dollars in real estate and I owned it all myself, and I thought I was invincible. I had the media come after me and I'd been on all the television shows that you can possibly imagine. And I had the Porsche and the BMW and the house on the beach and the whole thing when I was just nineteen."

In contrast to a generation raised in the 1960s when it was unfashionable in many quarters to quest for personal wealth, geeks for the most part find the idea unexceptional. Brian Morris (age 30), who left a large brokerage firm to start an investment company rooted in his African-American community, put it simply:

> *The point of personal wealth is important. . . . People say that "money is the root of all evil," but it's not. It's "[t]he love of money [that] is the root of all evil." And so there's nothing wrong with creating personal wealth. And if it's done right, ethically, morally, and done right in terms of its structure and how you are able to pass it on intergenerationally, then you are again creating that legacy that I was talking about.*

The contrast in aspiration and self-image between geeks and geezers is nothing short of dramatic. Geeks often strain to grab the brass ring on their first pass rather than waiting a few laps to get comfortable in the saddle. Their impatience is palpable.

Certainly their parents played an important role in shaping the geeks' self-image, but it wasn't just parents who urged them on. Television was a household staple for geeks—just as it was for their parents. However, unlike the simple (and often simple-minded) fare dished out by Howdy Doody and Huckleberry Hound, geeks were inundated with stories about adolescents and young adults who initiated (or were featured in) dramatic events, such as promoting disaster relief, rescuing stranded animals, simulating lunar landings at NASA space camps, testifying before Congress, or saving the planet through neighborhood trash cleanup. As the first children to have computers in the classroom, they were also gently nudged with reports about how nerdy youngsters like Bill Gates made a fortune before they had to shave regularly and how Steve Jobs and Steve Wozniak converted a garage hobby into Apple Computer.

Perhaps when you accomplish great things early in life, you don't change the nature of the journey, you just get to the end quicker. A case in point: Many of our geeks talked candidly about the pressures they'd felt and the damage they'd seen inflicted on others of their generation. By age 29, Michael Klein had more experience running (and closing) businesses than many executives twice his age, but he worried openly about the toll that "speed" and the promise of early wealth was taking on the people around him:

> *I see people all the time who are starting to crack up in this business. . . . Just not able to go on. Just reached the wall, if you put it in running terms, they hit the wall. They just can't go the last six miles or whatever it is. And they're bright, talented, capable people that in almost any other setting would be the stars of whatever company they would be in. And so I don't know what's going to give or what's going to change that. Because it's sort of built a culture and a momentum that doesn't really allow for any other way of doing things right now. But it's just not sustainable.*

Many Possible Careers

Geeks foresee many possible careers in a variety of work settings and many different models for relationships and families. They are engrossed in a life that more closely resembles an interactive computer game: more like the video game Sim Life than the board game of Life. In video games, players' roles are less well defined and can change over time. Key features of the game are revealed only through experimentation, and it's relatively easy to reboot if you don't like the way things are going.[7] For example, both men and women can have careers, and those careers may be complementary or antagonistic. Couples may hand career focus back and forth like a baton in a relay race. Marriage does not always precede career. Children may come before marriage—or without marriage or without a permanent partner, for that matter. Career may be a journey through many different jobs, as opposed to a lock-step progression within one field or one organization. Pensions do not always exist. Alternatively, many small pensions may need to be cobbled together to form an individual retirement scheme. Social Security may not exist or, if it does, it won't go terribly far. Retirement may go the way of Social Security, particularly if geeks live longer, continue to cherish diverse experiences, and remain economically, socially, and physically active beyond age 75.

The idea of "many possible lives" echoes an encouragement (some might say an admonition) that many geeks recalled from childhood: "You can be anything you set your mind to!" In a post–Title IX era, that admonition included girls as well as boys. Many possible lives also reflects the existence of a safety net—family inheritance—that largely did not exist for geezers. Not that geeks think a great deal about it, but many of the young men and women we interviewed could anticipate that inheritance—or, at minimum, financial backstopping from parents—would be there to support them if all else failed. Geeks measure success in terms of challenge, responsibility, and the opportunity to make history. Work is a form of self-expression. Entrepreneurship is an art form. For those who enter into dual-career marriages, there is always the possibility that one spouse can support career experimentation or risk-taking for the other. Not surprisingly, geeks expect to have nine different careers over a lifetime.

Speed

According to most geeks, a central feature of their era, if not the central feature, is speed. Jeff Wilke of Amazon painted a picture of what it meant to live and work in the 1990s that was shared by many of his peers:

> *So now all of a sudden you're in this period of wonderful trans-*
> *formation and we* know *it. I mean it's alive, it's tangible. Every*
> *day you sense that there's a chance to create new markets, to*
> *redistribute the players in the old markets as they shift over to*
> *the new one. . . . This company transforms itself on the order of*
> *months versus a number of years in an older, more established*
> *company. And the fact that you're reinventing yourself as a com-*
> *pany means the people associated with that company have to*
> *reinvent themselves.*

In a regime of rapid, often discontinuous change, geeks crave experience but believe they cannot rely solely on what Paolo Soleri earlier called the slow process of "acknowledgment." Over and over we heard young people thirsting for "twenty years of experi-ence in two years" and reminding those who labeled them naïve that, in reality, many people with twenty years' experience actu-ally had one year of experience repeated twenty times. Simula-tions, particularly complex computer-based models, make it pos-sible to formulate and test forecasts—to crank through alternative futures—at high speed and low cost relative to the cumbersome paper-and-pencil exercises that dominated business before the advent of the microprocessor. Case studies, supplemented by sim-ulations, are now the cornerstone of business school education.

Revered above all else are the lessons to be learned from "just going out and doing it." Entrepreneuring, like trekking, kayaking, mountain biking, and snowboarding, has become the avocation of young men and women raised to believe they can do anything and convinced that they live in an era without precedents. If con-ditions today are entirely new, why invest in old ideas and old methods of learning? Not surprisingly, therefore, people like Bill Gates and Earthlink founder Sky Dayton, who quit school to pio-neer new businesses during the dot-com frenzy, are often the poster children for the new way of getting experience.

Observing their rush to get experience, we began to wonder whether geeks approached learning in a fundamentally different

"So, Jim, where do you see yourself in ten minutes?"

way than the geezers. In one of our earliest interviews, Sidney Harman, 83-year-old chairman of the board of Harman International, said something that made us want to probe both geeks and geezers about their sources of inspiration. In describing the skills he thought leaders needed to cultivate, Harman argued forcefully for writing and reading: "One of my two favorite recollections in literature is Dylan Thomas's glorious phrase, 'The blank page on which I read my mind.' There it sits and today you write and the next day you read what you have written the night before and say to yourself, 'I'll be damned. I didn't know that I knew that.'"

Where do they go to get their intellectual batteries recharged? In the preceding chapter, we reported that geezers found succor and enlightenment in literature. Table 3-1 contrasts the reading habits of the two groups.

At first we were surprised by the rather disproportionate number of literary heavyweights showing up on the geezers' side of the column. When we probed, we found that geeks are reading the things that ambitious managers and executives in many circles—including many of the geezers—are reading: industry and trade magazines, daily business newspapers, online journals, and e-mails, hundreds and hundreds of emails. They also "read" the Internet, as Ian Clarke describes in the following sidebar. However, as we began to think about it, two hypotheses pushed to the

Table 3-1 **Favorite Works of Fiction**

Geezers	Geeks
• *The Emigrants* by W. G. Sebald	• *The Fifth Sacred Thing* by Starhawk
• *Diary of a Seducer* by Søren Kierkegaard	• Novels by Tom Clancy
• *On the Black Hill* by Bruce Chatwin	• *Watership Down* by Richard Adams
• Novels of Graham Greene and Evelyn Waugh	• *Catcher in the Rye* by J. D. Salinger
• All the works of Shakespeare	• *The Fountainhead* by Ayn Rand
• *The Woman in White* by Wilkie Collins	• *Atlas Shrugged* by Ayn Rand
• *Memoirs of a Geisha* by Arthur Golden	• *The Giving Tree* by Shel Silverstein
• *Huckleberry Finn* by Mark Twain	• Novels by James Michener
• *The Invisible Man* by Ralph Ellison	• *Pudd'nhead Wilson* by Mark Twain
• Novels by Charles Dickens	• *For Whom the Bell Tolls* by Ernest Hemingway
• *Anna Karenina* by Leo Tolstoy	
• *War and Peace* by Leo Tolstoy	
• *The End of the Affair* by Graham Greene	
• *The Grapes of Wrath* by John Steinbeck	
• *Holy Bible*	
• *Angela's Ashes* by Frank McCourt	

surface. First, curriculum reform in colleges and universities—a legacy of late 1980s campaigns to diminish the focus on Eurocentric perspectives—had eliminated many Western civilization and great literature requirements on college campuses. So, geeks had not read the classics because they'd not been required to. Second, in a digital, visual era, people haven't stopped reading, they've started viewing. Several of our geeks did admit to being avid moviegoers, but certainly not a majority. Most complained that they had precious little time left over after work, family, and community obligations had been fulfilled.

WHEN GEEZERS wanted to explore an idea or find a community of experts from whom they could learn, they journeyed to a library and pored through dusty stacks that often did not contain the promised reference source. For many geeks, the answers they seek are often only a few keystrokes away and communities of experts can be tapped with relative ease. Ian Clarke, 24-year-old founder of Freenet, talked about the impact of the Internet on his life:

I see myself as having been educated by the Internet. When I first went to university and I started to play with the Internet, I kind of got sucked into it. Not in the kind of sense that everyone kind of thinks, "A geek who can't socialize with people so they surround themselves with computers instead." I don't really subscribe to the view that that's what people are doing. I think I found myself learning from the Internet. The fact that you see something that interests you, maybe an academic paper. You can send an e-mail to the author of that paper and have a response within a couple of hours. The fact that you can find the answer to almost any question within minutes. All you need to do is state the question correctly. The fact that it's just this huge collaboration of people, many of whom are very, very smart, irrespective of geographic location. I think I view it as one huge university.

It turns out that geeks are active thinkers even though they may not be active readers, certainly not of classical or highbrow literature. However, instead of gaining intellectual nutrition from the classics, they are much more likely to engage in one of two activities: intellectual networking or passive, indirect reflection. Intellectual networking consists of active participation in discussion and debate with a carefully chosen group of peers. Often these networks are composed of classmates from college or an M.B.A. program and meet on a regular basis (annually or semiannually) to compare notes, discuss common problems, and react to outside speakers. The alumni network of MIT's Leaders for Manufacturing program (which includes Jeff Wilke, Elizabeth Kao, and Elizabeth Altman) is an example of this. In other instances, networks are much less formal. Passive, indirect reflection refers to time set aside for stocktaking and puzzling through issues that have been simmering for a long time in the context of another activity. Half the geeks mentioned that they got their best ideas while snowboarding, surfing, hiking, and/or camping (see the sidebar that follows). In some instances, these are solitary sojourns, but just as often they take place in the midst of others pursuing a similar form of recreation.

Why Be Loyal?

Geeks talk about experience in terms of experimentation and testing alternatives, as if life were like clothes shopping at the Gap. Far from being cavalier or feigning world-weariness, they adopt a tourist's attitude, because to them, the world is a constantly changing tableau. Moreover, a tourist's mentality ought not to be mistaken for dilettantism or an unwillingness to make commitments. In many respects, it is an understandable response to a world, especially a business world, where loyalty to an employer is neither assumed nor necessarily rewarded. Many of the young men and women we interviewed were adolescents in the 1980s and saw their parents and friends' parents "reengineered" out of

L IZ ALTMAN, 34, of Motorola, took up the issue of balance
as an essential element to creativity and innovation:

*I was working on my [master's] thesis and we were finishing
classes and interviewing for jobs and doing all this. I spoke to
a friend of mine who was about ten years older. I was explaining what was going on and she said, "So have you been
snowboarding recently?" And I kind of went ballistic. I said,
"SNOWBOARDING???? Do you understand? Have you been
listening to anything I've just said about what's going on in
my life??? I haven't written chapter two of my thesis yet and I
have ten interviews and these people are all annoying me and
I've got all these classes, whatever, and you're clearly not listening." And she very quietly said, "Liz, you've never worked
very well this way." And I was kind of annoyed and hung up
the phone.*

*Later, I thought about it and decided to go snowboarding
that weekend. . . . Kind of as a cliche, or corny as it sounds, I
figured out the major issue of my thesis while I was snowboarding because I wasn't thinking about it at all. And literally
halfway down the mountain I stopped and went "You fool!
Why aren't you thinking about it this way?"*

jobs in which they'd invested twenty or more years. The venerated
reciprocity between company and employee (especially white-
collar, managerial employee) described by Whyte in *Organization Man* crumbled in the 1980s even as management theorists
hallowed the Japanese system of lifetime employment. In the
remarkably resurgent economy of the 1990s, loyalty mattered
more to companies running short of key categories of professionals but less to those professionals themselves, because it was
their turn to ride the pleasant waves of a tight labor market (see
the sidebar that follows).

M ICHAEL KLEIN, the 29-year-old former CEO of eGroups, talked about the unique challenges of trying to inspire loyalty in an information-based company:

To me the biggest issue is that there's not any, not any bricks-and-mortar element, no assets, no buildings that you own, no processes that you own, nothing that you can lay your hands on. And then you have these prima donnas who walk out the door every night with everything that you own in their heads. Being able to convince those people that you are the company that they want to stay with is, to me, a twist on things. I mean you take a General Motors. Lots of people can walk out the door. They've still got a manufacturing plant. People go on strike, you know, they'll still own all their assets. If we had a breakdown of key talent walking out the door, we would be lost. And so in some ways, dealing with those very intelligent types of people who have this sense and understanding of their importance in the scheme of things, requires a huge dose of playing armchair psychologist and partner and coach.

Dan Cunningham, 26-year-old entrepreneur and self-proclaimed "Chief Chokolada" of Internet-based Dan's Chocolates, put the issue of loyalty squarely at the forefront of debate about experience and commitment. He recalled the advice of one particularly influential college instructor:

His message to us was, "Individuals need to realize that corporations cannot reward loyalty on a systematic basis. If the corporation falls on hard times, there are numbers and reasons that force it to make decisions that seemingly break the bond of loyalty and trust that employees may perceive to exist. Individuals need to make their own decisions with this in mind. And my

I'll give you an example that you never would have heard of at a company except in the information age. Our employees started complaining to us that we didn't party enough, that we didn't create an environment that was adequately fun for them. And I'm the same age as all these employees and I said to myself when I got this feedback—and I got it from twenty different sources—I said, "Since when is it the company's responsibility to create partying . . . ?" I mean, I'm not talking about a company picnic, I'm talking about an entire culture which is a social life for these people within the walls of the business. And we spent forty thousand dollars yesterday on a party for the employees that had rock climbing, human—what do you call them?—Sumo wrestling outfits, a band, the whole thing, and people said, "That's good. That's a first step. But you know all the companies out there, we're putting our entire lives into this thing and it's part of your job to create our social life too." And it's amazing, but they won't tolerate a lack of acknowledgment that they've put so much of their life into the business that we're also responsible for their social lives.

corollary on that is loyalty to individuals within a corporation must be maintained, but loyalty to the corporate entity itself may be a one-way street."

In a world where life expectancy has grown by 25 percent in seventy-five years, where technological change and globalization make every competitive advantage temporary, and where loyalty to employees (and vice versa) resembles historical fiction, it makes sense that status and career should be characterized by a continuous process of adaptation. Not one life, but many possible lives. Not one self, but many possible selves. Not a captive of history, but a maker of history. Not later, now.

Savvy and World-Weary

Beyond seeing the world (and their possibilities in it) through the lens of a television set, the geeks we interviewed have literally seen more of the world than any geezer had at a comparable age. What other group had seen a war unfold in real time? With its nonstop Internet and cable broadcast of battlefield action, video images from the nose cone of a smart missile, and live commentary on missile attacks from behind enemy lines, CNN presented Desert Storm with a you-are-there immediacy that Walter Cronkite never imagined possible. In the 1950s, families who took vacations outside North America were few in number; cost and a desire to stay close to home after having been gone for so long mitigated against grand global adventures. However, for the geeks we interviewed, foreign travel as a child was unexceptional. Not only had the cost dropped over time, but the bar had risen on what it took to impress one's friends. A friend who sits on the admissions committee of an elite private college told us: "A decade ago people were bragging on their college applications that they'd trekked through Europe or hiked in Alaska. Now they're talking about working in an AIDS clinic in Zaire, building homes for displaced peasants in Peru, and serving as guides in the rain forest."

Yet, for all their aspirations and achievements, the specter of paralyzing uncertainty occasionally loomed just beyond the optimism of limitless opportunities: If I can be anything and do anything, why be or do anything at all?[8] Geeks like Brian Sullivan, 29-year-old venture capitalist, may not have been paralyzed by all the choices, but they understood why some of their age peers refused to search for conventional careers even as they belittled their "McJobs" in suburban shopping malls. After college, Sullivan recalled taking a position he neither desired nor appreciated:

For me it was a way of having a job . . . and losing that scrutiny from parents whether I'm working or not. But I was not really applying myself. . . . I think I spent maybe seven or eight months

"Instead of 'It sucks' you could say, 'It doesn't speak to me.'"

at that job at the longest and just rationalized why it wasn't for me, why I should quit and what have you. . . . And about two months after that is when I realized, "OK, I quit," as opposed to finishing [what I'd started].

Another geek, a woman in her early 30s, summed it up nicely in a recent *New York Times* column: "I always swore I wouldn't replicate my parents' lives—a house in the suburbs, three screaming children, dinner at six every night—but now I think they might have been onto something. They weren't smothered in possibilities, as my generation is, and that was a blessing."[9]

This sense of being a very sophisticated kid in a very large candy store—facing delicious possibilities but sometimes wondering what the point is—was also reflected in the answers we got when we informally surveyed a group of twenty-somethings about the movies that best exemplified themes relevant to growing up in the 1980s and 1990s. Number one on the list was *Ferris*

Bueller's Day Off, the tale of a teenager who skips school, scams his parents and teachers, pulls off ingenious pranks, and best of all, gets away with it.[10]

Life in the Balance

No issue or attitude divided geeks from geezers more dramatically than the importance of balance in their lives. The desire for balance was a leitmotif in the interviews with younger subjects. One of the strongest advocates was Elizabeth Kao, 34-year-old product marketing manager in the Ford Motor Company. In a meeting of new managers, Kao asked then-CEO Jacques Nasser what the company was doing to facilitate their goal of achieving balance in their lives:

> *He threw it right back at us. "Well, I don't know. What do you guys think about it?" Basically his answer for himself was his choice for work/life balance may be different than ours, but it's a choice. And it took a lot of courage for our group to really stand up and say, "You know what? That is not what is happening at the lowest levels of your organization. This is not what it looks like. The emperor is wearing no clothes. This is not what it looks like in the trenches." And it takes a certain amount of courage to say, "No, it's not acceptable. When you're working seven weeks on straight, no days off. You ask your boss for a day off for your wife's birthday and he says no? It's not acceptable." So it takes a certain amount of courage to point out that kind of deficiency to the top guy in your organization, especially when you're pointing out, "Look, I don't want to work the same hours that you work." The expected reaction is the one from your other interviewee that says, "If you want to lead, forget about balance." I think that my group, my generation is rejecting that. If I can't do it with balance, then I don't want to do it. Or I'm not buying into your model of success.*

Dan Cunningham, founder of Dan's Chocolates, linked the idea of balance to his definition of being a successful person as well as a successful businessman:

> *I look at success in two areas, in my personal life and in my professional life. And I think a lot of people do break things down that way. But for me, by far the most important is my personal life. And I'm very careful not to let success objectives in my professional life intrude on the personal side. So I ask myself, Am I close to my family? Is my relationship with my wife strong? Am I staying in contact with friends? Am I doing community service on a regular basis? Those are things I really think are the most critical.*

Many of the geeks we interviewed shared Kao's and Cunningham's views, though only a few could summon up the passion of their arguments. More than a few—particularly denizens of Silicon Valley—worked long hours without respite or diversion as they chased their dreams of history and wealth. But even those who admitted setbacks in their effort to achieve balance still saw merit in the idea. For example, Lorig Charkoudian, the 27-year-old executive director of a community mediation program in Baltimore, described the paradox she encountered when she set about addressing the imbalance between work and personal time:

> *It's funny, because recently I was like, "OK, I've got to get more balance and figure out the different pieces of my life." I did a couple things that I've always wanted to do. I bought a motorcycle. Got my license. I love my motorcycle. I started training for a marathon. . . . And I recently started dating somebody that I actually like, which is unusual for me. And so I said, "I'm going to make that work. I'm actually going to carve out time for my life and that." And what I ended up doing is just not sleeping as much. So now I've gone from six hours a night, now I'm down to averaging four hours of sleep.*

Still, why all the commotion about the topic? And if balance is all that important, what are people *doing* to achieve balance?

To answer those questions, it helps to begin by recalling that the geeks we interviewed grew up at the height of the women's movement and during a time when many women were making deep inroads in a previously male-dominated labor market. In stark contrast to the geezers, whose mothers rarely worked outside the home, nearly all the geeks' mothers did. Geek families were dual-earner (often dual-career) families. And roughly three-quarters of mothers who worked outside the home held white-collar and professional careers. The majority of the young men anticipated that their spouses would also have careers.[11] In addition, nearly half of the geeks came from homes in which their parents had divorced by the time they were in high school.

In the Era of Options, the issue of balance became a very public one. Three factors elevated the debate. First, the growing number of women in management forced companies to rethink (though not necessarily to redefine) the traditional definition of career, strengthening the argument that a new balance is needed between the time devoted to work and nonwork pursuits (e.g., family). To be fair, balance is not just a women's issue: More and more men are questioning the assumption that they can get to know their children when they are teenagers. However, given that the household division of labor has yet to equilibrate and that management of child care remains fundamentally women's responsibility, corporate concern about balance has become another way of dealing with the growing number of women in management.

Second, the intensity of work in a digital economy has led geeks to search for ways to alleviate stress. At one level, extreme jobs encourage extreme sports. But more to the point, working in a 24/7 world takes its toll even when the rewards are high. More and more managers are being told that people want simply *to have a life* outside of work. Even in Silicon Valley, where work *is* life, organizational psychologists and human resource executives are urging high-paid talent to find nonwork pursuits in order to keep them fresh on the job. "Balance" is the euphemism for "get a life."

Third, extraordinarily tight market conditions in the late 1990s for professional and technical staff—the putative "war for talent"—led companies to search for new ways to make themselves more attractive. Even in a period of economic slowdown, key skills remain in high demand, and employers recognize that for many geeks an attractive compensation package must contain opportunities for learning sabbaticals, periodic travel for spouses and families to distant work sites, and redefined career paths to facilitate time for young children.

Something—time, commitments, authority, career advancement—has to give in order for balance to be achieved. Here we found evidence that some geeks are doing more than repeating a buzzword. For example, all the married men with children talked about strategies they'd implemented to insure they had time for their families. Jeff Wilke of Amazon.com and Sky Dayton, cofounder of Earthlink, talked with great conviction about the importance of being part of their children's lives. Wilke, for example, makes it a point to be home and involved with his family from 7 P.M. to 9 P.M. each day. Wendy Kopp talked about the rigors of leading a rapidly growing nonprofit organization and being a wife and mom:

> *I kill myself during the week so that I can have space on the weekends where I'm generally not dealing with work stuff. Whereas [before having a son] I used to be a little more sane during the week and just have a constant flow seven days a week. But right now, this seems like it's working. . . . I feel like I'm giving Teach For America the attention it needs. I'm giving my family the attention that it needs.*

Kopp sounds like a younger version of Shirley Tilghman (age 54), recently named president of Princeton University. When asked how she managed to juggle the responsibilities of being a professor, a lab director, and a single mother, Tilghman answered: "Brain compartmentalization. When I was at work, I thought about work. I did not think about the children. I did not feel guilty. When I left, I put on the Mom switch. I did not feel guilty."[12]

But balance means more than just time allocation or throwing the "Mom switch." Increasingly, it demands a different way of managing. For example, when asked how she made time for herself in the auto industry where executives traditionally devote fourteen hours a day to the job, Elizabeth Kao described her strategy for delegating and sharing responsibility with team members and direct reports:

> [I]f you have a leadership style where the buck, every single buck stops here and you have to be intimately involved with every single decision, then yes, I think that it is very easy to get off balance. I'm not going to let that happen to myself. Therefore I only have twenty-four hours in the day. I need to start empowering other people. I need to start, I need to trust my team that they're going to do what we agreed to: "You go do your thing. You agreed to take on this part, you go take it on. We'll come back together. But I'm trusting you to do your part."

Brian Sullivan, 29-year-old cofounder of Rolling Oaks Enterprises, a venture capital fund, admired the work habits of a CEO in whose company he had invested:

> He will leave the office no later than one minute after five every day. He gets into the office probably about six-thirty in the morning and he says, "I will get here as early as you want me to. A lot of our dealers are on the East Coast, and I'm happy to get here at six o'clock in the morning, but I'm not staying later than five o'clock because I need two hours a night with my kids." And that's it. And it's almost because of that dedication that we invested with him.

Although these accounts provide compelling evidence that geeks place great emphasis on balance, time will tell whether their efforts really do reshape the culture and conventions of corporate America. Half the geeks we interviewed were not yet married, and not all of those who were married had children. In that respect, they parallel their generational peers: The average age at birth of first child is 27, and our geeks are just approaching it. Still, with a few exceptions, even the unmarried, childless geeks expressed a commitment to balance in their work and nonwork lives.

The End of Heroic Leadership

We recall from the last chapter just how influential heroes were to our geezers during their formative years. Geeks, by contrast, don't have a ready list of heroes. They are flooded with business, sports, and entertainment celebrities—most of whom are depicted by the media, warts and all—but the people whom they consider heroes are more likely to be parents or others with whom they've had close personal contact or working relationships. When we asked each group to name their heroes, we got the responses shown in table 3-2.

The geeks' lists were dominated by their parents, although one young leader named the late Jerry Garcia of the Grateful Dead. A Web site called YourTrueHero.org showed a similar trend, with almost 40 percent of the mostly young people who logged on naming family members as their heroes.[13]

How do we account for the disparity regarding heroes in these two groups of leaders? What are the consequences for how each generation defines its motivation to lead?

Geeks grew up in an era of great institutional stability. This is not to say that social and political institutions are optimal or good; it is, however, to say that in the period of maturation for geeks, there have been few if any sustained challenges to the solidity of key American institutions from within or without. With the fall of the Soviet Union, the virtual hegemony of the American economy on a global scale, and an era of unprecedented economic growth, even flawed leadership is tolerated. The world in which geeks matured is a world dominated by celebrity, not by heroism. Politicians rarely became heroes and heroes only infrequently became politicians—but everybody could be a celebrity.

Table 3-2 **Heroes among Geezers and Geeks**

Geezers	Geeks
• Franklin D. Roosevelt (5)	• My parents (8)
• Ghandi (3)	• Friend or coworker (3)
• Abraham Lincoln (2)	• My grandfather
• Nelson Mandela (2)	• Hunter Thompson
• John F. Kennedy (2)	• Jerry Garcia
• Winston Churchill	• Roberto Clemente
• Alan Greenspan	• None or not considered
• Eleanor Roosevelt	relevant (6)
• Jean-Pierre Trudeau	
• Harry Truman	
• Martin Luther King, Jr.	
• Nelson Rockefeller	
• Jimmy Carter	
• Adlai Stevenson	
• Lao Tzu	
• Henry David Thoreau	
• Howard Baker	
• Beethoven	
• Mother Theresa	

The whole concept of hero, according to Elizabeth Kao, seems blown out of proportion, particularly when "every time someone gets nominated to be a hero somebody else comes along and reveals a dirty secret they have." The pervasiveness of information (whether it's accurate or not) renders heroes temporary and makes the idolization of individuals a risky business. Many of the geeks, ever-skeptical of hero worship, nonetheless expressed a longing for more people—especially, but not exclusively, public figures—whom they could respect deeply and for a long time. Perhaps to compensate for the lack of public figures worthy of that sort of regard, geeks chose people closer to home, people of less monumental accomplishments, but people whose accomplishments were tangible (perhaps even verifiable?) and who thus deserved their respect. Lingyun Shao, an Army reservist and trained nurse, explained:

> *I don't think I know people in public life well enough to make them my hero. I have a high criteria for people being my hero. Because I mean in public life, you hear about it through the press. Everything gets distorted. You don't really know them. I think I'd have to have a personal relationship with someone for them to be my hero. Like my advisor. I could consider her my hero because she's one of the only tenured women faculty members in nuclear engineering in the country, or in the world.*

Age, seniority, and rank no longer constitute *prima facie* evidence of accomplishment or expertise. Unlike geezers who at a similar age admired their elders, who were leading them to victory, geeks and the generation following them no longer see age as a dominant organizing principle. Sky Dayton made the case that the accelerating pace of change has made age irrelevant for everyone:

> *The cycle of innovation is so compressed now that it doesn't matter if you knew how to use a computer a year ago, because a year later it's all new again. So there's no more generation gap. It's just too new. And my son, who was four weeks old a couple days ago, is going to have to learn this stuff. . . . In his lifetime, the cycle will turn over so many times that it doesn't become an issue of age or generation; it just becomes an issue of viewpoint. Are you going to take on this technology and use it? Or are you not going to?*

What happens when technological change rapidly obsoletes skill bases (even for young people!) and electronically mediated communication routinely prevents people from knowing the age of the person with whom they're chatting? Obviously there are risks associated with such unqualified interaction, but it bears repeating that several of our geeks, including Geoff Keighley, 21-year-old founder and editor of GameSlice, an online interactive gaming review Web site, started their business careers as teenagers because the Internet did not require an ID.

The absence of heroes and larger-than-life icons among the geeks bespeaks an unintended side effect of the information revolution, including the Internet. Geeks and their younger siblings demonstrate a degree of sophistication and worldliness that is disconcerting. It's not just the dark rings under the eyes of those who work around the clock to make history or personal wealth that's disturbing. Instead, it's the recognition that because of the World Wide Web and instantaneous access to news (including speculative news, like the Drudge Report) society has become much more transparent—and so much more visible to so many more people at earlier and earlier ages. It's not just a matter of finding technological fixes, either. Certainly it's possible to install software filters on the home PC to prevent a 10-year-old from accessing pornographic Web sites. But the fact is that all you've done is inoculate one PC; there are still hundreds available in other people's homes, Internet cafes, dormitories, libraries, and classrooms that allow you to get from Google to Britney Spears to graphic sex and violence in three mouse clicks. Pornography is an extreme example, of course. But in an era in which, as one of our geeks, Ian Clarke (24-year-old inventor of Freenet), reminded us, "Knowledge wants to be free," then it's not likely that heroic individuals or images will last for long without being smattered with innuendo, libel, or misinformation.

Finally, in a society as complex and technologically sophisticated as ours, the most urgent undertakings require the coordinated contributions of many talented people working together. Whether the task is building a global business or growing a social movement, it doesn't happen at the top, however gifted or heroic the person at the top is. So, in many respects, it's understandable that geeks should be the first to let go of the myth of the Lone Ranger—the belief that great things are accomplished by a larger-than-life individual shouting commands, giving direction, inspiring the troops, decreeing the compelling vision, leading the way, and changing paradigms with brio and shimmer.

Now, in the Era of Options, an era of complexity and change, when aspirations for remaking the world are high, the sense we got from geeks is that real heroes are the leaders who work with followers as intimate allies. Intimacy and trust—the criteria that determine for geeks who is a hero and who isn't—cannot be achieved when leaders distance themselves from followers or when leaders allow themselves to be distanced. There is a delicious irony at work here: At a moment in time when it seems like anyone can become a celebrity, heroic leaders may very well be the men and women who shun the spotlight and put followers first. In conversation with geezer Don Gevirtz, geek Michael Klein offered this insight on the challenge of leading in an era such as this:

> *There are some big cultural differences, I think, between the way people need to be led in my generation versus past generations. Because people have been able to compress time frames so much and compress their road to monetary success so much, there need to be reasons for them being led that go beyond just the fact that they're punching the time card or coming in. They have to believe that they are changing the world, almost to that extent.*

The old command-and-control leadership is passé, as is the methodical decision making described by the U.S. Army acronym OODA—observe, orient, decide, and act. Instead of commanding, today's leaders align, create, and empower (ACE). Instead of taking action at the end of a process that begins with observation and reflection, today's leaders succeed in a high-speed environment that requires them to act first, then learn and adapt. The speed of the modern workplace is disorienting for some older leaders, though not the most vital ones. Chaos isn't just a theory, it is the current reality, and learning to live with, even love, it is an essential element of leading today. As General Electric CEO Jack Welch remarked recently, "If you're not confused, you don't know what's going on." In a sense, the difference between the old-style organization and the new is the difference between golf and surfing. Today, you need to be able ride the breaking wave of

Table 3-3 **Geezers' and Geeks' Concerns at Age 25–30**

Geezers' Concerns	Geeks' Concerns
• Making a living	• Making history
• Earning a good salary	• Achieving personal wealth
• Starting and supporting a family	• Launching a career
• Stability and security	• Change and impermanence
• Working hard and getting rewarded by the system	• Working hard so you can write your own rules
• Listening to your elders	• Wondering if your elders got it wrong
• Paying dues to the organization	• Deciding where loyalty should lie
• Using retirement to enjoy life	• Achieving work/life balance

constant change even if you can't see the shore or the sky. History and precedent probably won't help you.

An era insinuates its way into the lives of everyone who survives it, but most indelibly marked are those who come to maturity in its embrace. When you compare key themes from the interviews (see table 3-3), era-based differences stand out clearly. Geezers and geeks did not stand for opposed or contradictory things at the same age as much as they were trying to find their bearings in very different times. Geezers felt themselves reaching for a stable handhold after a period of instability and scrabbling. Geeks, on the other hand, looked to be reaching for higher limbs in the tree with an innate assurance that either they wouldn't fall or that someone or something would be there to catch them if they did. An interesting paradox, in other words: Geezers at roughly age 30 were striving to put instability behind them, while geeks were impatient to shake things up.

The end of this chapter also marks a transition in the book. As we pointed out in the introductory chapter, our initial interest in this project was anchored in a cross-generational comparison. We are now ready to take up the critical questions that only occurred to us as we ourselves became steeped in our study:

- How do exceptional men and women—young, old, and in-between—learn to lead?
- How have the geezers sustained their passion for leading?
- What does it take to lead for a lifetime?

We turn now to answering these questions.

FOUR

Crucibles of Leadership

TARA CHURCH, one of our geeks and founder of Tree Musketeers, encountered her crucible on an outing with her Girl
Scout troop. We were spellbound as she told us how she started
the only nonprofit in the world run by children, an organization
that has planted more than a million trees since 1987. As crucible
stories so often are, hers is a tale of transformation that has the
power and resonance of a fairy tale. Church recalled:

> California was in the middle of a very severe drought at the time,
> and we were going someplace that had very little water. And [the
> adults] were encouraging us to conserve it whenever possible.
> My mother was our Girl Scout leader [and she told us we had to
> decide if we wanted to use paper plates]. As we did with all
> issues, we sat in a circle and discussed the pros and cons, and
> then my mother mentioned the fact that using paper plates meant
> that trees have to get cut down. . . . And then she mentioned that
> there is this problem with deforestation and rain forests being
> massacred at alarming rates, and that led to a discussion of how

trees hold soil in place and how they filter pollutants from the air and there is this hole in the ozone layer. And she had this terrifying story, which we still haven't verified, that scientists were researching ways for the human race to live underground after the atmosphere is gone. And this all because there were not enough trees. . . . It was terrifying. It was the first time in my life that I remember being absolutely terrified. . . . All of a sudden I felt I was suspended in all of the horror of the world. This idea of living underground and not ever seeing the sunlight again, not being able to play soccer, climb trees, all of these things. I thought I was with this mass of dying people, and, at the same time, I felt utterly alone. It was really horrible. And then we had an idea, and our idea was that we should plant a tree. So we did. We planted a tree. And that was the single most empowering experience of my life. Realizing that while terror, while challenges, while all of these roadblocks can obstruct our view of what lies ahead, something so simple as getting a shovel and digging a hole and putting a tree in it can change the world. And I could do that. I was eight years old.

In this chapter, we will look at how our geeks and geezers and other leaders were transformed in their very personal crucibles. We will examine the nature of crucibles and what takes place in them.[1] And we will focus on the key competency that all leaders, young and old, have in abundance—adaptive capacity. But before we tell more stories, it might be helpful to review our model of transformation again, as shown in figure 4-1.

Think of Tara Church's story, and you'll see each of these elements in play. A child of her time, with a vivid sense of how precious and fragile the Earth is, she is confronted with a terrifying vision of what thoughtless consumption of natural resources does to the planet. But unlike those less imaginative, less hardy souls who are reduced to morbidity by the prospect, Tara has qualities that allow her to find meaning in the crisis. Instead of an ecological apocalypse, she sees reason for hope and a course of action— the wholesale planting of trees. The qualities that allow her to become a leader, despite her youthfulness, are strengthened by her

Figure 4-1 **Our Leadership Development Model Elaborated**

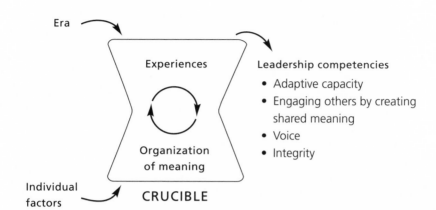

assuming a leadership role in creating the new organization, better preparing her for future successes.

Judge Nathaniel R. Jones of the U.S. Court of Appeals for the Sixth Circuit and one of our geezers, was transformed by the same process in a very different crucible: his interaction with a splendid mentor. As a teenager in Youngstown, Ohio, Jones "could have gone a very different way," he recalled, if it had not been for J. Maynard Dickerson, a successful attorney and editor of the local African-American newspaper.

Dickerson influenced Jones at many levels. The older man brought Jones behind the scenes to see how the great civil rights struggle of the 1950s was being waged, an experience that no doubt influenced the many important opinions Judge Jones has written in regard to civil rights. Dickerson was both model and coach. His lessons covered every aspect of Jones's intellectual growth and presentation of self, including schooling in what we now call emotional intelligence. Dickerson set the highest standards for Jones, especially in the area of communication skills—a facility that we've found to be essential to leadership. Dickerson edited Jones's early attempts at writing a sports column with respectful ruthlessness, in red ink, as Jones remembers to this day.

Dickerson also expected the teenager to speak correctly at all times and would hiss discreetly in his direction if he stumbled. Great expectations are evidence of great respect, and as Jones learned all the complex, often subtle lessons of how to succeed, he was motivated in no small measure by his desire not to disappoint the man he still calls "Mr. Dickerson." Dickerson gave Jones the kind of intensive mentoring that was tantamount to grooming him for a kind of professional and moral succession—and Jones has indeed become an instrument for the profound societal change for which Dickerson fought so courageously as well. Jones found life-changing meaning in the attention paid to him by Dickerson, a conviction that he, too, though only a teenager, had a vital role to play in society and an important destiny.

The Importance of Individual Factors

We have said little so far about one element of our model, individual factors, shown in the bottom left of the diagram. Since we devoted the two previous chapters to the eras of our geeks and geezers, we should explain why we are going to deal only briefly with the role individual factors play in creating leaders.

By individual factors, we mean "the hand you're dealt," the givens that any one of us brings to his or her encounters with the world. Traits and other individual factors have been among the most studied elements in the history of leadership. They are the essence of the argument in favor of the view—fallacious, we believe—that leaders are born, not made. If we were going to study the impact of class on the making of leaders, which we are not, we would include class under the rubric of "individual factors." It is undoubtedly true that, historically at least, being born male, white, and wealthy greatly increased the odds that an individual would achieve success, as both society and most individuals define it. That has certainly been the pattern in the United States, where leaders still tend to be male, white, and wealthy, despite affirmative action. But while those factors may be typical of the pool from which most current leaders come, they are largely irrelevant to the actual process of becoming a leader that we saw repeated over and over again. Wealth, for example, may smooth the way for high achievement, as it did for Franklin Roosevelt and John F. Kennedy. But it is no guarantee of it, as evidenced by the large number of wealthy nonentities in the world. Great intelligence helps individuals more often than it hinders them. But the only thing a high IQ is truly predictive of is an ability to solve the kinds of problems featured on IQ tests.

Much the same can be said for other factors often assumed to guarantee success. We found that most are significant only to the extent that they motivate or inhibit the individual who displays them. In theory, being gorgeous never hurts. In practice, it can paralyze a person as surely as it can benefit him or her. Our study confirmed our belief that traits and other individual factors are given far too much prominence in studies of leadership. Such factors rarely determine an individual's ultimate success. Leadership is much like other forms of creativity in this regard. The person who appears to hold the best genetic or socioeconomic hand doesn't necessarily win. The classic example is that of Poincaré and Einstein. Their mathematics professors would no doubt have predicted that the universally esteemed polymath Poincaré would have been the most important scientific thinker of his time, not Einstein, who looked, at least on paper, like a minor talent at best. There have indeed been great leaders whose emergence seemed inevitable as a result of their genius or some other fixed or genetic quality. But more often, success, including the kind of success we label leadership, emerges as a result of an individual's ability to adapt to a crisis or challenge (the event or situation we call a crucible).

Adaptive Capacity Is Key

To the extent that any single quality determines success, that quality is adaptive capacity. If you were underlining key points in this chapter, that sentence is the one that should be swiped with yellow highlighter. When we look at who becomes a leader, we see enormous variance in IQ, birth order, family wealth, family stability, level of education, ethnicity, race, and gender. Certainly these factors cannot be dismissed entirely. But in studying both very young and older leaders, we found over and over again that much more important than a person's measured intelligence—to take just one factor—was his or her ability to transcend the limits that a particular IQ might impose. In the case of intelligence, this includes avoiding the trap of seeing oneself as highly intelligent, hopelessly average, or below average to the exclusion of other, more useful self-definitions. We emphatically agree with Ford's Elizabeth Kao that "everyone has their own wall to climb." And we believe that both the willingness to climb those walls and the ability to find ways to do so are the real measure of a leader.

Yes, adaptive capacity, which includes such critical skills as the ability to understand context and to recognize and seize opportunities, is the essential competence of leaders. But adaptive capacity, as we discovered in studying our geeks and geezers, is also the defining competence of everyone who retains his or her ability to live well despite life's inevitable changes and losses. It is no accident that psychiatrist George Vaillant called his analysis of the findings of the famed Grant study (in essence, a description of the stages of adult male development) *Adaptation to Life*.[2] The Grant study examined the lives over many decades of 268 Harvard men, chosen as undergraduates between 1939 and 1942. (As in virtually all health studies of the period, women were regrettably excluded from the sample.) These men—in a very real sense, the brothers of our geezers—were chosen for their promise and relative mental and physical health because the psychiatrists and others conducting the study sensibly believed that science had tended to focus on illness so exclusively that we had failed to learn much about health. A crucial finding of the Grant study—one of the first to describe normal rather than abnormal psychology in adults—is that "soundness is a way of reacting to problems, not an absence of them." Like our geezers, the men of the Grant study encountered countless setbacks, heartbreaks, and difficulties, from the loss of loved ones to life-threatening illnesses. But the healthiest of the Harvard men adapted to these crises; they didn't break. And those successful adaptations, including one man's discovery and acceptance in mid-life of his homosexuality, allowed them to continue to grow.

To use the terms of our model, people with ample adaptive capacity may struggle in the crucibles they encounter, but they don't become stuck in or defined by them. They learn important lessons, including new skills that allow them to move on to new levels of achievement and new levels of learning. This ongoing process of challenge, adaptation, and learning prepares the individual for the next crucible, where the process is repeated. Whenever significant new problems are encountered and dealt with adaptively, new levels of competence are achieved, better preparing the individual for the next challenge. For those who become lifetime leaders, this extraordinary process of transformation, which provides the individual with new tools and new skills, leading to more success and more growth, occurs over and over again. It is the process that has already distinguished our geeks from their less impressive contemporaries, and it is the process that will allow them, over time, to become distinguished geezers.

Early in 2002 Vaillant published a sequel to *Adaptation to Life*, entitled *Aging Well: Surprising Guideposts to a Happier Life from the Landmark Harvard Study of Adult Development*.[3] This new book is based not just on the life experiences of the original Harvard study men but on those of gifted women and inner-city men as well. Some of Vaillant's most interesting new material describes the way the women, though hobbled by an era that limited their professional opportunities, adapted to their often mundane lives. One useful strategy a number of the women used was to rewrite their pasts in ways that downplayed the inequities they had experienced, allowing them to feel more useful emotions than the bitterness to which they were entitled. Like our study, the Harvard study found that the people who aged most successfully had great adaptive capacity, continued to learn new things, and looked forward, with eagerness and optimism, rather than dwelling on the past.

As we describe how the lives of our geeks and geezers were transformed in their personal crucibles, we will see the same thrilling process take place again and again, a process of change and growth that prepared each of them for future challenges and continued growth. Although none is a Pollyanna, all our geeks and geezers saw their crucibles, however punishing, as positive experiences, even as the high points of their lives. As we'll show, they not only survived their struggles, they were inspired and strengthened by them.

Aldous Huxley once observed: "Experience is not what happens to a man. It is what a man does with what happens to him."[4] Even though Huxley's pronouns date him, he is right. The extraction of wisdom from the crucible experience is what distinguishes our successful leaders from those who are broken or burnt out by comparable experiences. In every instance, our leaders carried the gold of meaning away from their crucibles. And they emerged with new tools as well. One invaluable take-home lesson to be learned from our geeks and geezers is that testing, however dire, is the hard but fertile soil that leads to continued growth, the process that liberates us from the past. As Vaillant so aptly writes in *Adaptation to Life,* "It is not stress that kills us. It is effective adaptation to stress that allows us to live."[5] No matter how terrible their crucibles, our geeks and geezers wasted no time ruing them. They all said, in essence: "I wouldn't have missed it for the world."

Real-World Validation of Our Findings

One of the reasons we trust the findings about leadership that emerged from our study was that we saw the same dynamic at work in the lives of leaders outside the study. Although Arizona senator John McCain was not one of our geezers, his is a superb example of the transformational power of adaptive capacity. Imprisoned by the North Vietnamese in the notorious Hanoi Hilton, McCain was part of a group of heroic American soldiers who found ingenious ways to best their jailers. In spite of torture and isolation, the imprisoned men quickly created a code that allowed them to communicate. Their jailers never managed to intercept the prisoners' messages, relayed via a code that used taps, coughs, and other nonverbal signals, because the prisoners built in a culturally based security system their guards never figured out. When a prisoner wanted to send a message, he tapped out "shave and a haircut." If the prisoner heard only "shave and a haircut" tapped in response, he knew there was a jailer at the other end. Only his fellow Americans knew to add two final taps for "two bits." One fearlessly clever prisoner, forced to make a taped confession that was subsequently shown in the United States, repeatedly blinked the word *torture* in Morse code throughout his ordeal.

In the Hanoi Hilton, adaptive capacity transformed a desperate means of communication into a David-like triumph over a formidable enemy. Most accounts, including his own memoir, *Faith of My Fathers,* explain McCain's courage and leadership in terms of his family's almost Athenian tradition of honor, patriotism, and self-sacrifice (both his father and his grandfather were much-decorated United States admirals).[6] But we believe adaptive capacity was the crucial element that allowed him to survive a terrible captivity. It was unquestionably adaptive capacity of the highest order that allowed him to emerge whole from what must have been an almost unbearable crucible—his signing a confession of criminal war-mongering after a particularly vicious round of torture. Instead of easing his captivity, family tradition might as easily have crushed him when he could not uphold that tradition in his suffering. Duty may have faltered at a critical moment, but McCain's remarkable adaptive capacity allowed him to overcome his shame, perhaps even a belief that he had committed treason, and to enter a post-military life marked by an apparently happy family life and a distinguished career in public service.

In the mini-memoirs and sidebars in this chapter, you will get a rare glimpse of people as they are being tested and transformed.

The crucibles our geeks and geezers experienced varied enormously. Some, like Paolo Soleri's learning to climb mountains or Harlan Hugh's mastery of karate, might seem too mundane to bring about important change. Others, like Sidney Rittenberg's imprisonment, are experiences in which the individual is clearly at risk of sustaining permanent damage, even death. But whether the experience is the death of a loved one or immersion in an unfamiliar culture, all crucibles are events or experiences of great importance to the individual changed by them. *Crucible* is an almost infinitely elastic term that is ultimately defined by the person transformed by it. This is an important point. We truly know only one side of any conversation—our own. We know every tortuous turn and pang of our own ordeals and rites of passage, but we never know more than a cartoon version of anyone else's. Unable to hear my interior monologue, you may not realize that I am struggling at all—from the outside what I perceive as an ordeal may look like a charmed existence (see the following sidebar). In this sense, the journey that transforms an individual into a leader is always a lonely one.

JUDGE NATHANIEL R. JONES, nominated to serve on the U.S. Court of Appeals for the Sixth Circuit in 1979, chronicled his own struggle to craft a sense of self in the face of powerful external assumptions: "Lurking in the back of my mind at all times was a sense that I was always being underestimated. That I knew within myself what I wanted to try to be. And I felt that there were others that just sort of assumed that I could never achieve anything but what they expected me to be. And I wasn't going to let those limitations be my limitations."

Under the mentorship of Maynard Dickerson, a lawyer and newspaper publisher, Jones had the opportunity as a teenager to sit in on conversations with civil rights activists like Thurgood Marshall, Walter White, Roy Wilkins, and Dr. Robert C. Weaver.

And I would hear these lawyers and these activists as they would now be called, talking and discussing. And I was struck by their resolve, their humor, their approach. And their determination not to have the system define them. They provided the kind of rationalization that helped you get through it all and helped you develop what they would call and what I came to adopt as coping skills. In order to maintain your sanity and your sense of self respect, you had to devise means of coping with all of these assumptions that were out there about your inferiority, your unworthiness—that you're not good enough, that you can't achieve. And they gave the juice that helped you rationalize. And the thing that struck me was the sense of humor that they brought to this. Rather than anger, they brought humor. And they ridiculed people who practiced these stereotypes of superiority. They would talk about persons who were utterly amazed when they would find that a black person knew how to use a knife and fork. Or had manners. Rather than just feel beaten down, they turned it around.

Later in our interview, he recounted a story told by South African Bishop Desmond Tutu that touched him deeply:

He talked about the slave mentality and how, even today, many black people still have that slave mentality. . . . He talked about the residual effects of slavery and apartheid, what it has done to people, to the victims of the system. And he said it even affected him. And he gave a story about the time he was on a flight and he boarded the plane, and he noticed that the cockpit crew was black, and he thought that was interesting. And he took a seat and the plane taxied and took off and as they were traveling they hit some bad weather, hit a pocket and the plane began to bounce around. He said his immediate thought was, "I wish there was a white person in the cockpit, part of the crew." And then it hit him. He said, "My god, this is part of that mentality."

The journey is different for everyone, even when the basic facts are the same. Look at how differently Nathaniel Jones and James Conlon responded to the struggle for civil rights. Jones dedicated his life to the law and advancing equality. Not one of our subjects, Conlon is principal conductor of the Paris Opera and music director for the German city of Cologne. Like Jones, Conlon met Martin Luther King, Jr. briefly while still a youngster. But instead of turning him into a civil rights activist, Conlon told *Harvard Business Review,* King's example "constantly prodded me to go beyond the inborn self-centeredness of the artistic soul."[7] King also inspired Conlon to abandon the harsh teaching methods of his own teachers, "who focused on my imperfections, provoking feelings of inadequacy in me." That Jones and Conlon should experience King so differently is not surprising. As we discovered, every leader finds, or creates, the meaning he or she needs in the crucible.

The Difference between Fasting and Starving

Crucibles vary in duration (and in anticipated duration), in harshness, and in other ways. But there are two basic types: the ones you seek and the ones that find you. There is a world of difference between the two—the difference between jumping into an abyss and being pushed in, between fasting and starving, between emigration and exile. Some of our leaders had their crucibles forced upon them—Sidney Rittenberg's sixteen-year imprisonment may be the cruelest example. The majority of our leaders chose their crucibles, although rarely with a full understanding of what the experience would bring. Some, such as Arthur Levitt, Jr., became seekers of crucibles, constantly looking for the kinds of challenges that would stretch them. In a career of more than fifty years, Levitt served in the Air Force, was both a cattle broker and an editor at *Look* magazine, and served under President Clinton as chairman of the U.S. Securities and Exchange Commission. "What I believe is important in life is to keep as many doors open as possible," Levitt explained. "You close a door when you fall in love with a community and say you won't move. . . . I'll move any place. I couldn't care less where. . . . And I think that's important. You re-pot yourself."

Jack Coleman also consciously sought out tests and challenges. Now owner-editor of a weekly newspaper in Chester, Vermont, he has been a professor of economics, chairman of the Federal Reserve Bank of Philadelphia and president of Haverford College. But he is best known for taking time out of his privileged routine to experience the blue-collar lives of a garbage collector, a dishwasher, a prison guard, and an auxiliary police officer. He also lived for ten days on the streets of New York—a harsh crucible, reminiscent of George Orwell's experiences "down and out in Paris and London," but one that Coleman knew would end when his sabbatical was over and he returned to campus.

Whether imposed or sought out, crucibles are places where essential questions are asked: Who am I? Who could I be? Who *should* I be? How should I relate to the world outside myself? These are always places of reflection, but they are typically places where one transcends narrow self-regard and reflects on the self in relation to others. They are often places where one becomes increasingly aware of his or her connectedness. They are also places of choice, even when the choice is narrowed, as it was for Rittenberg and the long-imprisoned Nelson Mandela, to retaining or losing one's human dignity in the face of those who would strip it away. Crucibles are, above all, places or experiences from which one extracts meaning, meaning that leads to new definitions of self and new competencies that better prepare one for the next crucible.

The terrorist attacks on the United States on September 11, 2001, were an imposed crucible of the cruelest sort. We don't know how most of the thousands of people who experienced that event were changed. But we saw a vivid example of one man who seemed utterly transformed in Howard W. Lutnick. As head of the bond-trading firm of Cantor Fitzgerald, Lutnick would normally have been at his desk on the upper floors of the World Trade Center when it collapsed after being struck by two hijacked jets. Instead, he had taken his 5-year-old son to his first day of "big-boy school." The 40-year-old executive arrived at the trade center that morning just as the attacks began. Inside were 1,000 employees of his firm. Six hundred died in the attacks and subsequent collapse, including Lutnick's 36-year-old brother, Gary.

We know what Lutnick was like before—a tough trader, with what the *New York Times* described as a "flinty edge."[8] Known for his steel, not his compassion, Lutnick responded to the catastrophe by reaching out to the families of his employees. He wept openly in television interviews and gave his private home phone number to the families of every employee. Before the day was out, he had set up a family services center in a nearby hotel. "We have a new class of partners here—these families," he told the press, with tears in his eyes. By Thursday, the company was back doing business in makeshift quarters, and Lutnick had donated $1 million to a newly created Cantor Fitzgerald Foundation, to aid the families of anyone who died in the attacks, whomever they worked for. Later, angry members of the families of Cantor Fitzgerald dead would excoriate Lutnick for promptly sending out paychecks stamped "final" to their survivors. But whatever the ultimate truth, within hours, Lutnick seemed to have measured himself against a new reality and emerged different from the man he was before.

Crucibles are inevitably places where people play for mortal stakes. The test is often grueling, whether it is an institution-sanctioned rite of passage like Officers Candidate School or a novitiate. There is always a prize, whether it is the promise of freedom that kept Sidney Rittenberg alive or the promise of power that allows some of our geeks and geezers to endure the rankling orthodoxies of government service and corporate life. There is always a real chance of failure—you don't know while you are in a crucible how the story is going to end or what your fate is going to be. But all our leaders saw their crucibles as propitious moments, dangerous perhaps, but also rich with opportunity. They believed, as FDR said in his second inaugural address: "This generation has a rendezvous with destiny." And even though our geeks and geezers knew they could fail, they had the optimist's expectation that they would win. They saw an arc to a desirable future that they believed they could travel. They were convinced that the goal was worth the struggle and that they would prevail.

Our study dealt only with people who had passed through their crucibles and had emerged stronger and surer than before. If that were the universal experience, it would not be worth writing about. As we all know, while everyone is tested, some people fail. They learn nothing in a potential crucible, are broken in it, or emerge confused and demoralized. But to a person, our geeks and geezers came through in good psychological health, ready and able to tell their tales.

Adaptive Capacity as Applied Creativity

In essence, adaptive capacity is applied creativity. It is the ability to look at a problem or crisis and see an array of unconventional solutions. Adaptive capacity includes the quality Keats found essential to the genius of Shakespeare—negative capability. This gift, the poet explained in an 1817 letter to his younger brothers, is evident "when man is capable of being in uncertainties, mysteries, doubt without any irritable reaching after fact and reason."[9] Those with negative capability may have considerable regard for fact and reason, but they also realize the wisdom of entertaining opposing views at the same time. John Gardner, for example, was able to see the past as "ballast and a teacher" and, at the same time, to realize that conventions and habits are limiting as well as comforting. "Beware," he said, "of the prisons you build to protect yourself."

We spoke earlier of the gift our leaders have for thriving in chaos, for tolerating ambiguity and change. Studies of creativity by psychologist Theresa Amabile indicate that creative people are not only more tolerant of ambiguity than others, they also are able to consider multiple options for a longer period. They don't rule out possibilities prematurely and so they are able to make better, more artful choices. They can tolerate the nettle of uncertainty in situations where others long for closure. Most of our leaders have the requisite hungry patience to seek untested paths. But they also have the discipline necessary to achieve a desired goal. Even as they value unorthodoxy and change, they also finish dissertations and get M.B.A.s because they know that such well-worn routes to success, even when they are tedious, are often worth the payoff.

Sidney Harman, octogenarian entrepreneur, former college president, and Carter cabinet undersecretary, showed a leader's attitude toward risk when he talked about the difference between recklessness and daring:

> *You proceed recklessly when you make no provision at all for an understanding of what the odds are or what the consequences are. You then must blindly move ahead, whether it's in a life decision or business decision. . . . Daring for me is an action you take understanding that the odds perhaps are against success, but having examined the whole network, understanding what the odds are, reckoning what the consequences can be, you make a judgment that "I'm prepared to proceed against that knowledge."*

Flexible, resilient people are not repelled by problems; they pounce on them, determined to find solutions to the puzzle, however painful they may be. Adaptive capacity allows individuals to confront unfamiliar situations with confidence and optimism. Those with well-developed adaptive capacity are not paralyzed by fear or undermined by anxiety in difficult situations. They believe that if they leap, a net will appear—or, if it doesn't, they will be able to find or fashion one in time. Where others see only chaos and confusion, they see opportunity. Bill Porter, who founded E*Trade in 1982, long before it was obvious that people would some day want to trade stocks at the speed of light, is a perfect example. "When you see a situation," he says, "you *go* for it."

Another example of someone who saw opportunity in chaos is 30-year-old serial entrepreneur Sky Dayton. Asked if there was a particular point when the idea of Earthlink arrived, he thought for a moment and then laughed:

Wow, you know, there was. I was trying to get onto the Internet, and I had a book that I bought on how to do it, and I had an account that I'd gotten from an Internet service provider, and I had a Macintosh computer. And I spent eighty frustrating hours, banging on the computer, calling and trying to get help, not getting any. . . . I was tearing my hair out; it was horrible. I was sort of hacking my way through the jungle. And when I finally got connected, it was like I had arrived at this clearing in the jungle, and there was this golden pyramid, and I had a vine hanging around my neck and a leech stuck to my forehead. And so, some moment in late 1993, three A.M., when I finally made the thing work and I'm sitting at home, and I'm looking at this thing, and I'm like, "OK, this is it." A light bulb went off in my head: "I'm going to make it easy for anyone to get to this. And I'm going to bring the mass media to the masses." And that was it. I dropped everything else I was doing.

For Porter and Dayton, as for Thomas Edison and other giants of adaptive capacity, failure is a friend, not an enemy. When things don't turn out as they had hoped, they transmogrify failure into something palatable, even desirable. They see approaches that don't work not as something shameful, but as sources of valuable information that will eventually lead to a successful outcome.

Adaptive capacity allows people to embrace and explore new technologies, rather than demonize them. Former General Electric CEO Jack Welch is a good example. After initial resistance to using the Internet, Welch not only became an enthusiast, he assigned an electronically sophisticated geek to each of the company's 4,000 top managers. The compensation of the executives was linked to how readily they learned the skills taught by their young mentors. Indeed, seeking out expertise, wherever they find it, is one of the strengths of almost all our geeks and geezers. Our geeks tend to be stalkers of first-rate mentors. Our geezers don't hesitate to tap the wisdom of their children and grandchildren.

Old or young, our leaders have the ego strength to admit that there are things they don't know and to see learning as a reciprocal process. As Embark.com cofounder Young Shin put it: "We realized that we didn't have a lot of the operational experience we needed, so we brought in some senior managers. We had a lot to learn from them. But, at the same time, we knew some things they didn't, and we were proud of the things we knew."

Like other creative people, those with powerful adaptive capacity inevitably take pleasure in the problem-solving process. No matter how terrible the dilemma may be—a serious illness, a sick dot-com, an unjust and brutal imprisonment—grappling with it and finding a solution becomes a source of satisfaction, even pleasure. As the process of problem solving floods the person's brain with pleasure-giving endorphins, dealing creatively with the problem becomes both motivator and reward. The more a person uses his or her adaptive capacity, the stronger and more supple it becomes. (We will say more about adaptive capacity and the other competencies of lifetime leaders in the next chapter, in which we will flesh out the rest of our model depicted in figure 4-1).

The crucible is the occasion for real magic, the creation of something more valuable than any alchemist could imagine. In it, the individual is transformed, changed, created anew. He or she grows in ways that change his or her definition of self. How do we know that people are changed? Often an observer can see the difference, but more important, the individual perceives it.

The crucible is a dividing line, a turning point, and those who have gone through it feel that they are different from the way they were before. In explaining how she had been changed by an early entrepreneurial failure, Ford's Elizabeth Kao recalled that she was at a "crossroads," a decision point at which she could either continue on the same less-than-satisfying road or "jump to the next plateau." When pressed about what happened in the crucible, each of our geeks and geezers explains that he or she has acquired new insights, new skills, new qualities of mind or character that make it possible to function on a new, higher level—to "jump to the next plateau."

In the course of testing, the individual makes choices—to take a chance, to be selfless, to take responsibility, to start something new, to do the right thing. And when the testing is over, he or she emerges convinced that they were the right choices. This sense of having made personal choices that led to growth gives the individual a new, more generous self-perception. Believing that they have been transformed or have transformed themselves, those who survive the crucible are more confident, more willing to take future risks. That new self-confidence is grounded in the belief that he or she has done something hard and done it well.

Don Gevirtz (founder of Foothill Financial Group) spoke about this process in describing his initiation as ambassador to Fiji:

I'd been confirmed by the Senate and I got on the airplane with my wife and we flew out to what was a life-changing experience in Fiji. And also one that was very frightening in many ways. Frightening because the rookie ambassador walked into this place with instructions and approval from the State Department and the NSC to deal with human rights abuses that had occurred there, and in my first press conference, I was critical of the government and the human rights abuses. And I learned there what persona non grata meant. It meant that because the government was so angry at me, their government, that they were thinking of throwing me out of the country before I had a chance to get settled, unpack my bags in the wonderful ambassadorial residence. But eventually, in working closely with the prime minister and members of his cabinet, we were able to draw close together and work well as a team, the prime minister and his people, to build a really major record there. By the time I left, they had passed a new constitution, constitutional reform that I had sought and worked for behind the scenes and out front.

Many of our geeks and geezers had already prepared themselves for their crucibles by contemplating alternative selves. Success is, first of all, an act of the imagination. Whatever their age, our leaders realized that they were not limited by the roles they had played in the past or the ways they had been defined by parents, teachers, or others. Our leaders have never been mired in the "now." Many have long been in the habit of dreaming about things they might do, a habit often acquired early in life. Jeff Wilke credits his stepfather with opening his eyes to worlds outside of blue-collar Pittsburgh. Because of his stepfather, Wilke considered schools other than nearby Penn State and careers other than his beloved baseball. Fantasizing about becoming a professional baseball player was Wilke's first step in transcending the givens of family and class (as dreaming of playing pro football was for Legacy Unlimited founder Brian Morris). Wilke's stepfather encouraged him to widen his repertoire of possible futures.

Seeing the World in a New Light

A crucible is a tipping point where new identities are weighed, where values are examined and strengthened or replaced, and where one's judgment and other abilities are honed. It is an incubator for new insights and a new conception of oneself. Often the transformational event in the crucible is a realization that one has power that affects other people's lives. One of the life-changing lessons of any battlefield—or any medical school, for that matter—is that other people's lives are in your hands. Mike Wallace recalls how, during World War II, he was struck by the realization that American submariners depended for their very lives on his performance as a communications officer. Parenthood is another common crucible that makes one acutely aware of sobering power, responsibility, and interconnection.

While an undergraduate at the University of Michigan, with thoughts of becoming an English teacher, CBS News reporter Mike Wallace happened upon the campus radio station and discovered that his distinctive gravelly voice worked well in news reporting.

He literally "found his voice" in Ann Arbor, Michigan. But it was Navy duty in World War II that taught him the power of voice.

> *In the Navy you had a chance to think about yourself and what you wanted to do when you got back . . . and it turned out, the Navy turned out to be a remarkable chance to take a look inside yourself. What is it that you want to be? Mind you, I was still in my twenties. But what do you want to be? You're 26 years old, 27 years old. Only in retrospect do you realize that that's what you were doing. But the Navy gave me a chance, gave me a pause to think about it. . . . All of a sudden you were in the position, forced into the position of being in charge, not just of yourself, but in charge of a job. And I was a communications officer. Started as an ensign. Wound up as a JG. But suddenly I'm playing with strips or the ECM machine and talking to the boats, the submarines out on patrol. And god damn it, I'm in charge! I was in a position of genuine responsibility.*

The crucible makes the individual see the world in a new light. In the *Harvard Business Review,* civil and human rights activist Eleanor Josaitis recalls "to the exact moment, when my life changed."[10] It was 1962, and she was an affluent housewife, 30 years old, raising five children in an all-white Detroit suburb. That evening, she was watching footage of the Nuremberg trials on TV when the show was interrupted with news of police using dogs, fire hoses, and cattle prods on peaceful civil rights marchers in Selma, Alabama. "I kept asking myself: 'What would I have done if I had lived in Germany during [the Third Reich]? Would I have pretended that I saw nothing?' . . . I also wondered: 'What am I doing about my own country?' I immediately became a strong supporter of Martin Luther King."

Josaitis found, or made, meaning where most others saw only tumult. So profoundly was she changed that she sold her house, moved to an integrated urban neighborhood, and devoted herself to racial justice. She never looked back, even when her mother tried to have her five children taken away from her and she was disowned.

The ability to find meaning and strength in adversity distinguishes leaders from nonleaders. When terrible things happen, less able people feel singled out and powerless. Leaders find purpose and resolve. In the crucible, to paraphrase former British prime minister Margaret Thatcher, iron enters the soul and turns to steel. Vernon Jordan was belittled and, instead of lashing out or being paralyzed with hatred, he saw the fall of the Old South. His ability to organize meaning around a potential crisis turned it into the crucible in which his leadership was forged. Jeff Wilke experienced this transformation after a workplace tragedy (see the sidebar that follows).

The Hero's Journey

Whatever the crucible experience—going into battle, overcoming fears, entering unknown territory—the individual creates a narrative around it, a story of how he or she was challenged, met that challenge, and became a new and better self. The story is the one at the center of every myth—the hero's journey. In a sense, our geeks and geezers have become their own heroes. The process is not necessarily a conscious one. But, whether they know it or not, our leaders all agree with writer Isabel Allende that "you are the storyteller of your own life, and you can create your own legend or not."[11]

Our leaders, young and old, have all chosen to create their own legends. Not fakes or phonies, all our leaders have "authored" a true version of their lives. The improved self that is the protagonist of this new story is so admirable and authentic that others recognize the newly minted hero or heroine as extraordinary. The crucible produces a leader both in that individual's own eyes and in the eyes of others. So confident is the changed individual in this new vision of self that he or she often feels compelled to share it with others. It is important to remember that ours is a dynamic model—what is learned, including the learning of learning, drives and prepares the individual to repeat the process, to go farther, to learn and accomplish more.

T HE ABILITY to extract wisdom from experience is a skill honed in the crucible. Quite often, the lessons learned are as much about values as they are about leadership. Jeff Wilke, 33, had been a general manager responsible for a facility where an employee was killed. His reflections on the experience illustrate a lesson he learned about values as well as leadership.

I had the horrible misfortune . . . we did as a business, of having one of the employees at a chemical plant that I was responsible for die on the job. And the soul-searching that you go through when that happens about "How could this happen? Who's responsible? Or are we in some way responsible?" And you start to question all these things. And to go to the town, to meet his widow, to speak at the plant, to spend a week with these folks and to understand their pain and to try to help them through what's happened—it just, it's a transformational experience. I mean in terms of the importance of leadership.

. . . [Y]ou can convince yourself, I think, in an industrial environment that leadership is about making money, making the quarter, making a sales target, and at the end of the day you get to go home to your nice cushy, you know, urban or suburban life style. But to realize that in the end it's all these lives that are all wrapped up together, and every so often an event happens that isn't just about whether we made the quarter...it hits you square in the face.

Wendy Kopp recalled the process of reflection and resurrection that gave birth to the idea of Teach For America:

I was in this funk and I started thinking, "You know, I'm not alone. There are thousands of graduating seniors out there who are just searching for something that they're not finding and really want to make a difference in the world." And then one day

I thought of this idea: Why doesn't this country have a national teacher corps that recruits all these people who are dying to do something that really matters, to teach in urban and rural public schools? And that's where we really need their energy. I mean I literally just became obsessed with that idea, and thought, "This is such a powerful thing. Not only would these people have a huge impact during their two years, but I had this idea that this would change the consciousness of the country. That it would shape the consciousness of all these future leaders who would go on to do lots of important things."

All these elements—the lesson being learned, as well as the lesson about learning—are present in the story told us by young Motorola executive Liz Altman, who believes she was transformed by her stay in Japan, and so she was. Like many initiates, she began her transformational experience uncertain, even fearful, of what lay ahead. It was, Altman says of her year working in a camcorder factory in rural Japan, "by far, the hardest thing I've ever done." In addition to the loneliness she felt in an alien culture, she had to carve out a place for herself as the only woman engineer in a plant, and nation, where women are usually assistants and other subordinates, known as "office ladies." Before Altman arrived at the plant, she had been warned that the only way to win the respect of the men was to avoid allying herself with the office ladies. But when the women graciously tried to include her on her first day, she chose to ignore the warning rather than insult the women. She used the comfortable respite created by that choice to closely observe the unfamiliar culture of the office.

Thanks to what we recognized as her considerable emotional intelligence, Altman found a way to break with the women without alienating them and a way to link up with a few of the men—fellow engineers—using the pretext of their common interest in mountain bikes. Ultimately, she became good friends with the department secretary—one of the women she had instinctively chosen not to alienate on her first day. That woman, the wife of one of the engineers, went out of her way to make sure Altman was included in social events and other activities from then on. "Had I just gone to try to break in with [the men], and not had her as an ally, it would never have happened," Altman said.

Altman looks back on the experience as one that gave her an invaluable education and that prepared her for much of what was to come: "It was really valuable in teaching me to just stop and think and learn and watch what's going on and try to—adapt to the culture is probably not really correct because you're not going to adapt—but [to] be able to perceive what's going on and learn to watch and learn to not go by all your previous assumptions." Her tenure in Japan taught her to observe closely (to be a first-class noticer) and to be slow to jump to conclusions based on stereotypical cultural assumptions. She learned to do that reflexively, she says, and those are skills both she and her employer say are invaluable in her current work at Motorola, where she helps smooth alliances with other corporate cultures, including those of Motorola's different regional operations.

With the model in mind, let's look at two of our other geezers in their crucibles.

Elizabeth McCormack has had a long and distinguished career as an educator and leader of various philanthropic organizations. As an educational leader, she was president of Manhattanville College during the tumultuous period from 1966 to 1974, when campus unrest swept the country and her own institution redefined itself, largely through her efforts. Her philanthropic work has included heading the Rockefeller Foundation, serving as vice chair of the John T. and Catherine D. MacArthur Foundation, which grants the so-called Genius Awards, and serving as head of the Atlantic Foundation.

McCormack is keenly aware of the impact her era has had on her life. She was, she recalls, a child of the post-war 1940s, born into a well-to-do, traditional Roman Catholic family in which girls went to Catholic colleges, if they went to college at all. Looking back, McCormack wonders if she decided to become a nun because, in her heart of hearts, she did not share her parents' very conventional dream for her—that she marry a nice Catholic boy, have children, and live in the suburbs. Instead, McCormack became a sister of the Order of the Sacred Heart, which she remained for thirty years. The hand that McCormack was dealt included a vigorous intelligence, robust health, and other assets that have served her well over the years. But it is her adaptive capacity that allowed her to emerge as a leader and to continue in that role after she left the convent and married. Optimism, self-confidence—the whole gestalt of life- and health-affirming attributes that social scientists call "hardiness"—are important elements of that adaptive capacity.

So, too, is McCormack's ability to seize the opportunities presented to her. Although most outsiders think of a religious order as a place devoted solely to prayer, contemplation, and good works, it is also an organization that has to be run. And, unlike so many traditional organizations, convents are run by women—women who do not have to compete with men for leadership positions and who both mentor and are mentored by other female leaders. McCormack had taken a vow of obedience, and so she took whatever positions her superiors told her to take. But when, for instance, she became the headmistress of a Connecticut boarding school, she both learned the principles of leadership on the job and put them into practice. At first, at the age of 30 and with little or no executive experience, she felt woefully ill prepared to head a school. But in part by remembering all that she had disliked in the management style of a nun whom she had served under earlier, McCormack was able to develop her own leadership skills. She discovered that one way to create a great organization is to hire people who are so good at their jobs that they may be a threat to your own. She also discovered that the leadership style she excelled at, and the one that gave her the greatest satisfaction, was unleashing the potential of other people—a selfless style that a leadership-savvy friend called the "no fingerprints" approach.

In a sense, McCormack's entire thirty years as a nun was her crucible. But there were times when she was tested more severely than at others. One time of testing—and of growth—was when she decided, in the mid-1960s, that Manhattanville had to reinvent itself in light of cultural changes, or die. Her own alma mater,

Manhattanville had long been the Catholic equivalent of a Seven Sisters school—an elite college that attracted the best and the brightest of young Catholic women. But, in part because of the new ecumenism fostered by Pope John XXIII's Second Vatican Council, more and more talented Catholic girls were being lost to secular institutions. That trend would only accelerate when, in 1967, Yale became the first of the formerly all-male Ivies to accept women. McCormack knew what had to be done and, after winning over her board of trustees, led the school to a new identity as a secular, coeducational institution. But it was a painful process. One angry alumna sent McCormack a postcard with a picture of a stained glass window showing Judas betraying Christ with a kiss. "This is you!" the woman had scrawled on the card.

Another of McCormack's formative moments had taken place earlier and may mark the point when she acquired the confidence in her own judgment that led her to leave the order, despite her sacred vows. As a young nun, she was sent to study St. Thomas Aquinas at Providence College. She obeyed, of course, and learned Thomistic philosophy as well as anyone, but she felt, in her heart, that the 700-year-old teaching had little application to the world she knew. When she was tested on the teachings of St. Thomas, she answered each question with the prescribed response but prefaced her answer by saying: "I have been taught at Providence College that . . . " No fool, the president of the college confronted her and asked her if she meant by that prefatory phrase that she didn't believe her answers. "That's right, I don't believe them," she told him. "You're honest, but you're wrong," he told her. "I'm honest, and I'm right," she said only to herself.

Often our leaders are aware of an exact turning point or defining moment in their journeys. "That was a turning point," McCormack recalls. It was the moment she found her voice, even if she wasn't yet ready to use it. In McCormack's case, it is hard to sort out exactly when she began to define herself as someone who was not a nun. But fairly early on, her personal moral compass took her in a direction unsanctioned by her faith of record. She recalled that she was once approached by one of her students at Manhattanville who said her sister, a junior in high school, was pregnant.

Afraid that their father would kill the sister if he found out, the student asked McCormack if she would help arrange an abortion for the teenager. "Of course," said McCormack, who knew the father and believed he was deranged. "I had no problem with that," McCormack recalled. In McCormack's protracted crucible, a definitive change had occurred between the time she could speak her independent mind only to herself and the moment at which her personal perception of what was right trumped her vow of obedience. She eventually came to believe she could live the life she wanted only outside the order, in a community of two called marriage, working for the common good in secular organizations. Part of her healthy adaptation to this new life is her ability to see her convent experiences as invaluable ones that enriched her life, rather than as wasted years. With enough adaptive capacity, there are no failures, only growth.

Few crucibles are as clear-cut as the one that turned Sidney Harman into a pioneer of participative management. Founder of audio giant Harman International and deputy secretary of commerce under Jimmy Carter, Harman recalls that he was holding down two executive positions—heading his own firm and serving as president of Friends World College—when he had his defining moment. It was in 1968, Harman recalls, a time of political unrest across the country, when he was told that there was a crisis in the Bolivar, Tennessee, plant.

At the time, Harman says, the Dickensian factory was a "raw, ugly and, in many ways, demeaning facility." The problem erupted in the Polish and Buff Department, where mostly African-American workers did the dull, hard work of polishing one car mirror after another, often under unhealthy conditions. The men on the night shift were supposed to get a coffee break at 10 P.M. When the buzzer that announced the break went on the fritz, management arbitrarily decided to sound another buzzer at ten minutes after ten o'clock. But one worker, Harman recalls, "an old black man with an almost biblical name, Noah B. Cross," had what Harman describes as "an epiphany." "He said, literally, to his fellow workers, 'I don't work for no buzzer. The buzzer works for me. It's my job to tell me when it's ten o'clock . . . I got me a watch. I know when it's ten o'clock. I'm not waiting another ten minutes. I'm going on my coffee break.' And all twelve guys took their coffee break, and, of course, all hell broke loose."

At this point in Harman's account, he explains that Friends World College was an experimental Quaker school whose essential philosophy was that students, not their teachers, were responsible for their own education. Harman was juggling the two jobs, living what he calls a "bifurcated life," changing clothes in his car and eating lunch as he drove from plant to campus. The worker's refusal to be cowed by management's senseless rule was a revelation to Harman. Noah B. Cross don't work for the buzzer, the buzzer works for him. Cross's principled rebellion changed Harman's life. He had one of those moments of insight, a click in the head that changes everything: "The technology is there to serve the men, not the reverse," Harman remembers realizing. "I suddenly had this awakening that everything I was doing at the college had its appropriate applications in business." Harman subsequently made the plant more like a campus—offering classes there, including piano lessons, and encouraging the workers to take most of the responsibility for running their workplace. Participative management wasn't a grand idea conceived in the CEO's office and imposed on the plant, Harman says. It grew organically out of his going down to Bolivar "to put out this fire." The Harman after Bolivar was a different animal from the Harman before, first in his own mind, and then in the eyes of the world. Harman's transformation was, above all, a creative one. He had connected two seemingly unrelated ideas and created something new—an approach to management that recognized both the economic and humane benefits of a more collegial workplace. His insight continues to transform workplaces around the world.

As Harman recalled his long and distinguished career, we were vividly aware that he had taken the bare facts of his life and fashioned them into a rich and resonant story of which he was the hero—and rightfully so. He had found meaning, and direction, in the crucible of Bolivar, meaning that he was able to communicate to workers throughout the firm. Harman's response to what was happening in Bolivar was a classic example of an able leader's ability to grasp context—another key aspect of adaptive capacity. In dealing with the crisis at the plant, he also evidenced at least two of the qualities seen in leaders who succeed in galvanizing others through shared meaning. He both empathized with the workers and encouraged dissent. A vehicle for the latter was the plant's lively independent newspaper, the *Bolivar Mirror*. Harman understood that, painful as it may be, dissent is useful information. He also valued the paper because it allowed the workers to express themselves, giving them a creative and emotional outlet that he clearly believes in, for both business and humanitarian reasons. Workers enthusiastically skewered him in the pages of the paper, Harman says. However, it is clearly a source of satisfaction to him that when *Forbes* magazine ran a piece about his being the second highest paid CEO in the country that he was "largely teased about it in Bolivar, not assaulted for it."

All our leaders have learned how to learn and to keep on learning. Elizabeth McCormack says that she and a talented friend who often flew together would make it a point to read the book the other was reading on the plane. Enormously thoughtful and insightful, Harman also takes his lessons where he finds them. Harman says that he learned an important lesson from the example of his longtime friend, former President Carter. When Harman observed the president in meetings, Carter always seemed to know more than anyone else. But no matter how much interesting information was exchanged in those groups, Harman recalls, "it was rare for one of those meetings to produce a leap of imagination, a leap of faith, a truly creative leap." That prompted Harman to try to be "the kind of leader who sees himself not as the ultimate wisdom, but as one who acts as the catalyst. His role is to cause the others to reach beyond their normal capacity, to invent something they hadn't brought to the meeting, something *no one* had brought to the meeting." In this, Harman was like the exemplary leaders of creative collaboration that Bennis and Biederman describe in *Organizing Genius*.

Harman says that he learns more from writing than from almost anything else. "I learn much more about what I think, how to think, because I write and because I'm respectful of writing, and because I read what I've written, and read it critically." He also says that he sees curiosity as one of his defining characteristics. The octogenarian says he can't imagine getting up in the morning with the intention of just getting through the day. Two of the attributes he treasures most are "curiosity and humor. If I were obliged to select only two characteristics, I would forego nobility. I would probably forego courage. If I could only have two, they would be those two, and I value humor very, very highly."

The transformation that our leaders described when they talked about their crucibles was essentially a process of education. Learning how to learn was one of the most valuable tools they took away from their crucible experience, and it was one of the all-purpose tools, along with creativity, that they depended on in all their subsequent dealings with people and the world. In order to thrive, Dee Hock told us, you need "a deep love of learning and a refusal to be anywhere that didn't let you learn or prevented you from learning." For Hock, as for many of our other leaders, commitments should be made on the basis of the educational potential of the person or situation. It is the likelihood that you will learn something worthwhile, not prestige or stock options, that makes a particular work situation attractive. The change that our leaders experienced—the thing that pushed them to the next plateau—*is* learning, and they all seem to appreciate its unique power.

The Lessons Taught by Failure

The curiosity that Harman so values is the engine that allows him to continue learning, that keeps him taking chances and taking on new challenges. Like many of our other leaders, his love of learning seems to have anesthetized him against fear of failure. He understands that you may not get what you want when you take a risk, but you will always learn something. That view takes the sting out of failure and makes it something worthwhile and meaningful. As Harman told us, "The whole point of failure is to learn from it." This redemptive view of failure is that of artists as well as other kinds of leaders. Harman's curiosity is what keeps him jumping again and again into the crucible described in our model that results in more learning, more change, more growth. Many of our geeks and geezers saw their eagerness to learn and grow as their most fundamental and precious asset. An exemplary lifetime learner, Don Gevirtz studied Eastern philosophy as intensely as he studied annual reports and leapt fearlessly into an unfamiliar culture when he became ambassador to Fiji when almost 70. He told us that he wanted his tombstone to read: "He grew."

Let's look at how some of our geeks negotiated failures. Elizabeth Kao, after a childhood of precocious achievement and academic success, started a dot-com with college friends. The young partners believed they had "*the* killer app," Kao recalls, until they found themselves so broke that they had to bribe the power company into leaving the electricity on so they could hold a meeting. When Kao became so worried about unpaid bills that she couldn't sleep at night, she made the painful decision to give up her business and go to management school. Unaccustomed to failure, the then 22-year-old had to face her limitations as an entrepreneur. Instead of brooding, she did what the resilient do: She recast disaster into something of value—a hard but important lesson. "It made me realize that I'm possibly a little more risk-averse than I had initially thought," she says. Optimistic and upbeat even as she was being severely tested, she was able to appreciate her strengths at the same time that she acknowledged her weaknesses. "During that time I found out some good things about myself as well . . . tenacity, perseverance, as well as the innovation."

At Ford, Kao is able to express the risk-taking side of herself in a relatively stable corporate environment. Adaptively, she has found a place for herself within the giant automaker as one of its least conventional managers, a role she clearly relishes. "I like the rebels," she says. "My friends are mostly rebels within my company. People who are willing to shake things up. Maybe people who have courage. It's something that I value very much in my group of friends, and they in turn give me courage to do the hard thing or to do the right thing."

Michael Klein's adaptive capacity allowed him to reinvent himself repeatedly before he turned 30 in 2000. At 19 he lost $20 million when the real estate market tanked. The teenage business prodigy found himself with a single asset, a tiny software company he had acquired because he had liked its financial analysis software when he had used it in his real estate business. He built that company into Transoft, which was acquired by Hewlett Packard in 1999. He also created eGroups, a service that allows individuals with a shared interest to meet electronically, which he sold to Yahoo! in 2000 for $432 million. A major reason Klein has succeeded in one enterprise after another is that he long ago learned how to learn. His grandfather, Klein's mentor since he was 5, was a business school of one, and, Klein says, he usually spoke to his grandfather on the phone for an hour every day until shortly before he died.

Klein continues to react quickly and optimistically to changes in the economy and his own fortune. We interviewed Klein with finance innovator Don Gevirtz, then in his 70s, on the day in 2000 that the Nasdaq plummeted. Both men had lost millions in the previous twenty-four hours, but their psychological hardiness was evident as they spoke eagerly of future opportunities, confident they would succeed again. Our leaders all respond nimbly to new challenges. Elizabeth McCormack and her husband, Jerome Aron, have always loved music and going to concerts. Since he has lost much of his hearing, they have devised a new strategy for dipping into the cultural treasure trove and now devote more time to reading.

In the next chapter, we will delve deeper into the powerful role that neoteny plays in the development and sustaining of leadership.

But for now, let us say only that every one of our geezers is what we began to call a neotenic, someone whose vigor and openness to new experience marks him or her as the antithesis of stereo-typed old age. We realized that neoteny is also a useful metaphor for the vibrancy that characterized our younger leaders as well. To a person, they too are full of energy, full of curiosity, full of confidence that the world is a place of wonders spread before them like an endless feast.

FIVE

The Alchemy of Leadership

WHAT ALLOWED Sidney Harman to face a factory revolt and discover in it, not chaos, but a radically new way to empower workers? How did Tara Church, only 8 years old, find the inspiration for a thriving nonprofit in a downbeat discussion about paper plates?

In reviewing the videotapes of all our geeks and geezers, we found the answer to these questions again and again. In the previous chapter, we talked about crucibles and the critical role they play in shaping leaders. All our leaders, whatever their age, brought to their crucibles four essential skills or competencies. These are the attributes that allow leaders to grow from their crucibles, instead of being destroyed by them. In every case, the quality most responsible for their successful navigation of these formative experiences was their adaptive capacity—an almost magical ability to transcend adversity, with all its attendant stresses, and to emerge stronger than before. Every one of our leaders had three other essential qualities as well: the ability to engage others in shared meaning, a distinctive and compelling voice, and a sense of integrity (including a strong set of values). In this chapter, we will talk more about each of these competencies and show how they contribute to the alchemy of leadership.

Some of our leaders had other gifts as well, such as technological virtuosity, but these four—adaptive capacity, the ability to engage others in a shared vision, a distinctive voice, and integrity—were the sine qua non of all our successful leaders. Once we identified these essential leadership qualities, we realized that these are the qualities of leaders in every culture and context. They are the attributes that sustain and define leaders, not just in our digital age, but in every era, every public arena, every business and boardroom.

Adaptive capacity is what allowed GE's Jack Welch to transform himself from staff-slashing Neutron Jack into Empowerment Jack as the needs of the corporation shifted. The ability to engage others through shared meaning is what allowed a mediocre tactician named George Washington to inspire the Continental Army to defeat the better equipped but less well led forces of King George. A fine physicist but previously undistinguished administrator named J. Robert Oppenheimer found his distinctive voice long enough to provide inspired leadership of the Manhattan Project, cajoling, counseling, and buoying his secret community of scientific geniuses as they raced to insure that the Nazis did not make the first atomic bomb. And all these leaders possessed a powerful moral compass of the same magnetism that inspired millions to follow Gandhi and Martin Luther King, Jr.—a quality we will refer to as integrity.

It became clear to us early on in our study that these qualities—the Big Four, as we came to think of them—were repeatedly underscored in the interviews with our geeks and geezers. They comprised their winning combination. In the elaborated model shown in figure 5-1, we illustrate each of the four basic competencies, plus related abilities.

In this chapter, we will show how these crucial attributes helped shape the leadership of our geeks and geezers and other leaders. We will underscore the importance of these qualities by looking at flawed leaders. And we will also talk more about the process that produces leaders—the alchemy of era, individual

Figure 5-1 **Our Complete Leadership Development Model**

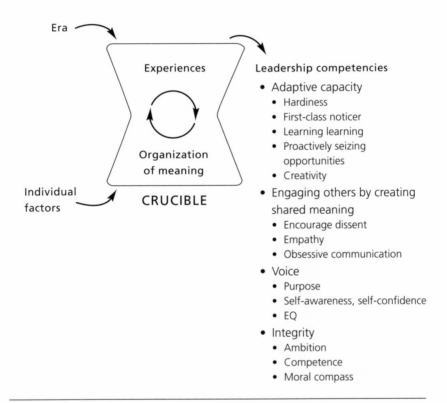

factors, and leadership competencies that allows leaders to emerge from the defining experiences we call crucibles.

It is important to note, however, that an individual may have the requisite qualities for leadership and little or no opportunity to use them. Who knows how many people with the necessary gifts for extraordinary leadership are stifled by class, racism, and other forms of discrimination, including the *burqa*. However gifted, great leaders emerge only when they can find the proper stage, a forum that allows them to exercise their gifts and skills. In the eighteenth century, Britain's restless American colonies produced half a dozen superb leaders as greatly talented individuals rose to a life-or-death challenge and grappled with a problem worthy of great minds—what form of government best suited a free people. Leadership guru Abigail Adams spoke of the importance of the crucible of history in shaping leaders more than 200 years ago when she wrote to John Quincy Adams in 1780: "These are the hard times in which a genius would wish to live. Great necessities call forth great leaders."

Great Necessities, Great Leaders

The surprise terrorist attacks on the United States in 2001 seemed to call forth just that sort of greatness. In the months before September 11, Rudolph Giuliani was the lame duck mayor of New York, best known as the hard-liner who had cleaned up the city. It was a reputation off-putting to many, and somewhat tarnished by his nasty split from wife Donna Hanover. But in the crucible of the attacks on his city, Giuliani was transformed. As the *New York Times*'s Frank Rich wrote of Giuliani a few weeks later: "At ground zero, he projected comfort as well as authority, tenderness as well as steeliness. In the midst of performing round-the-clock triage on a grievously wounded city, he even found the time to honor a commitment to attend a wedding and serve as an honorary father of the bride, in a tux no less, to the sister of a New York fireman who had died on duty in August."[1] Giuliani was tireless throughout the ordeal, recognizing and dealing with issues as varied as deferring visits to the massive crime scene by former President Clinton and others to finding out whether canon law would allow missing Roman Catholics to be declared dead before seven years had passed (the answer was yes). But it was his palpable empathy and his ability to communicate this consoling message—that all New Yorkers, and indeed all decent people, had been grievously wronged but would endure—that revealed his unexpected stature as a leader, prompting some of the same journalists who had once damned him to write rapturous tributes.

Even more dramatic was how President George W. Bush seemed to be transformed in the same crucible. Snatched out of harm's way immediately after the assaults on the World Trade Center and the Pentagon, he did not get off to a distinguished start. "Where is the president?" people wondered, and understandably so. But in a matter of days a president with an uncertain mandate and a less-than-memorable oratorical style had found his voice. On September 20, Bush gave a half-hour speech to Congress and the nation that approached greatness.

Many observers were stunned. In a piece in the *Wall Street Journal,* longtime Democrat Gerald Posner described a new George Bush, one who suddenly emerged to meet the challenge the country faced. "Like Franklin Roosevelt or Winston Churchill," Posner wrote, "he rallied a country's spirit, had the courage to tell us the bad news that the upcoming battle would be neither swift nor easy, and declared that those who would destroy our culture and values would not prevail."[2] Posner had previously found Bush to be a stiff speaker, especially when delivering a prepared text. But on this occasion, Posner said, "he was infused with passion and outrage. His sincerity was heartfelt, and boosted almost all who listened to him. And precisely because we all know he is not a masterful orator, the power of his words and the forcefulness of his delivery carried even more impact. He rose to this most important occasion."

As we said earlier, the fact that we repeatedly see our leadership model at work in the world bolsters our confidence in its validity. The president's speech showed all four essential competencies of leadership. The adaptive capacity that allowed President Bush to turn even his usual verbal awkwardness into a strength. A newly found and compelling voice that allowed him to engage an entire nation and its allies through shared meaning and common purpose. Moral conviction that gave his condemnation of the attacks the force of something more than political expediency. Like Abigail Adams, Posner recognized crisis as a powerful catalyst. "More often than not," he wrote, "real leadership flourishes when faced with imminent threats and dangers."[3]

Bush was acutely aware of the seriousness of the moment and was determined to seize it, yet another ability evidenced by our geeks and geezers. As Leo Braudy tells us in his classic study of fame, *The Frenzy of Renown*, Alexander the Great associated himself with nothing less than the gods when forging his imperial image.[4] In conversations with friends, President Bush confided that he was inspired throughout the crisis by one of the deities of the modern leadership pantheon, Winston Churchill. (Mayor Giuliani was similarly inspired by the legendary communicator, who buoyed Britain during the prolonged terror of the Blitz.) Indeed, at one point in tweaking Bush's address, speechwriter Michael Gerson sat with presidential counselor Karen Hughes in front of a plaque that bore Churchill's stirring line: "I was not the lion, but it fell to me to give the lion's roar." Although echoes of Churchill were heard throughout the speech, Bush insisted that no quotes from great leaders be included. As Bush made clear to his writers and advisors, he saw the speech as an opportunity to lead, and he wanted his to be the words the world remembered. The speech was wildly effective, winning the praise of Ted Sorensen, Ted Kennedy, and other non-Republican connoisseurs of the language of leadership. More important, in the course of delivering its 2,988 well-chosen words, Bush seemed to change before the nation's eyes from a down-home, easy-to-dismiss Prince Hal into something more akin to a home-grown Henry V.

Leadership is one of the performing arts, and the leader always has to sell himself or herself to the audience. That is precisely what the president did. At the risk of committing psychobiography, he appeared, in the course of thirty minutes, to shed his previous role of Fortunate Son and to assume a leadership role based on models that included but transcended his father. In the crisis and its aftermath, the president seemed, for the first time, to recognize that he would be judged by history. Following the speech, Bush's approval rating shot to 90 percent, the highest in the history of presidential polling, with a record 72 percent of Democrats expressing their support for his crisis management.

Bush's transformation was reflected in his behavior as well as his speech. Fabled for his devotion to downtime before the attacks, he was now in the Oval Office at daybreak, studying briefing books with an unprecedented seriousness. He stepped up his physical fitness regimen as if in training, upping his daily time on the treadmill and trimming the fat in his diet. He even assumed a new formality in his dealings with the other members of his administration, calling Secretary of Defense Donald Rumsfeld "Mr. Secretary" instead of the usual pre-crisis "Rummy."

As the attacks recede in time, a far more subtle and complex presidential leadership will be required than the martial style that worked so well immediately afterward. We will need a leader who can balance protecting freedoms with protecting the lives of the citizenry, and it is not yet clear who that leader will be. The same president who moved us with his eloquence could falter badly in such critical areas as encouraging dissent, not a strength of his administration before the events. But while the ground was still smoldering after the assault, the president seemed worthy of his office even to many who had voted for other candidates.

In an "etymology" of the speech in the *New York Times Magazine,* writer D. T. Max wrote: "War had given the president a second chance to define himself, an accidental shot at rebirth."[5] War has been one of the most demanding and most dependable crucibles for leaders at least since David won his kingdom by defeating Goliath, and Bush recognized and seized the opportunity it presented. War's ancient association with leadership may be why military metaphors are irresistible to football coaches and CEOs. But war does have all the qualities of a genuine crucible— the mortal stakes, the terrible risks, the pressures that force one to decide what is truly important and how one wants to live, the need for intelligence and courage, the potential for obliteration, and the opportunities for greatness. The "great necessities" of September 11 seemed to call forth greatness in George Bush, Rudolph Giuliani, and countless others, just as World War II unleashed the leadership ability of so many of our geezers, from John Gardner to

Mike Wallace. Whatever these post–September 11 leaders accomplish in the future will be achieved with the aid of insights and skills that they acquired in that horrifying, unexpected crucible. They will venture forth from a higher plateau, on firmer ground, as a result of that harsh education. At Ground Zero, as elsewhere, the competencies acquired in any one crucible prepare the individual for the next, in a great circle that allows higher and higher levels of learning and achievement.

Remarkable Adaptive Capacity

Although we talked about adaptive capacity at considerable length in the previous chapter, it is hard to overemphasize its importance in the creation of leaders. An exemplar in so many ways, Sidney Rittenberg outshone Houdini in his ability to overcome anything his captors threw at him. Rittenberg is hardiness incarnate, a remarkable embodiment of the ability to thrive in stressful situations so central to adaptive capacity. When years in isolation began to take an intellectual toll on him, he found inspiration in simple stories such as "The Little Engine That Could." Even more remarkable was the low-key way he dealt with his eventual release. He recalls his prison door suddenly opening in 1955, after his first six-year term in prison: "And here was a representative of the central government, telling me that I had been wronged, that the government was making a formal apology to me, that I was a good person and they had treated me wrongly, and that they would do everything possible to make restitution. He said, 'We'll give you money if you want to go back to the States and make a new start in something, we'll give you enough money. If you want to travel in Europe, we'll arrange that. If you want to stay here, we'll give you a nice villa somewhere and you can read and write and do whatever you like.' . . . I said, 'I want to go right back to doing the same job that I was doing on the day you came in that little jeep and arrested me.' "

People such as Rittenberg are models for Jeff Wilke, 34, who makes it a practice to seek out the hardy. "You know that Teddy Roosevelt quote about 'credit belongs to the one who is in the ring, whose face is marred by blood and sweat and knows the great passions and also knows the great failures,' " Wilke said. "I want to meet those people. I want to meet people who have thrown themselves into things and have something to say about it. And who have failed and have also triumphed while 'daring greatly.' . . . Those are the people I want to meet."

Perseverance is another component of hardiness and thus an aspect of adaptive capacity. Sky Dayton prides himself on being tough and says he psyches himself up to follow a course of action, however full of obstacles. "I can't tell you the number of people who told me I couldn't open a coffee house at 8205 Melrose," he recalls. "No way. Government guys with big stamps DECLINED, DISAPPROVED. My partner and I spent a week just pounding on the planning guy until we figured out a formula that was a loop-hole to the law that would allow us to do some really weird arcane thing, and the guy was scratching his head at the end, going, 'My God, you're right, I guess I have to approve you.' . . . Perseverance and toughness, it's really important."

How Not to Lead

As we have said before, bad leadership can be every bit as instruc-tive as good. We have talked about the four competencies of lead-ership and some of the qualities and capacities that contribute to each of them. You can sometimes best see those qualities in their absence. Another reason for discussing bad leadership—failed leadership is a kinder term—is that there is so much of it. These are demanding times, and many gifted individuals falter in them. The most visible failures are the ones at the top. Once a sinecure, the job of CEO has become a revolving door in recent years. The remarkable twenty-year tenure of GE's Jack Welch is even more noteworthy when compared with those of most recent CEOs, who seem to fail faster than laptop batteries. According to a 2000 study by the consulting firm of Drake Beam Morin, chief executive officers named after 1985 were three times more likely to be fired than those appointed before that time.[6] According to the same study, 34 percent of *Fortune* 100 companies had replaced their CEOs since 1995. This churn at the top is universal, not confined to the United States or to a single industry. Worldwide, the average number of CEOs was 1.9 in ten years. And the trend is toward replacing unsatisfactory CEOs ever more quickly, a reflection perhaps of more vigilant boards and the staggering levels of compensation paid chief executives—now routinely 300 times that of ordinary workers. In recent years, Mattel, Lucent, Rubbermaid, Campbell Soup, Coca-Cola, and Covad have all replaced CEOs in thirty-seven months or less. Heads of Gillette, Procter & Gamble, Maytag, and Xerox have been ousted after less than a year and a half.

As we have said, Shakespeare's Coriolanus is a cautionary tale on how not to lead. Despite his integrity and other virtues, Coriolanus was fatally lacking in both adaptive capacity and the necessary gift of engaging others through shared meaning. Adaptive capacity always includes the ability to grasp context. But unlike Saul Bellow's alter ego in *Ravelstein,* Coriolanus was a fifth-rate noticer.[7] He failed to notice that Rome was changing from a patrician state to one where the plebians also mattered. His mother, Volumnia, begged him to engage the crowd, to meet and communicate with his constituents. To do so, Coriolanus tragically believed, was to sacrifice his integrity in order to win over the mob. His bad leadership ultimately killed him.

Coca-Cola's Coriolanus

M. Douglas Ivester was the Coriolanus of Coca-Cola. Inheriting the chairmanship on the sudden death of its esteemed, long-time CEO, Roberto Goizueta, Ivester lasted just twenty-eight months. His grasp of context was woeful. Unlike his ethnically sensitive predecessor, Ivester failed to empathize with minority employees, so much so that he demoted the highest ranked African-American even as the company was losing a $200 million class-action suit brought by black employees. This in Atlanta, a city with a powerful African-American majority.

This lack of emotional intelligence was not Ivester's only flaw. He also failed to grasp the importance of his presiding over the European negotiations for Orangina and responding promptly and personally to the discovery of adulterated Coke in France. Worst of all, he didn't have the ego strength to acknowledge his interpersonal weaknesses and name a second in command with a defter touch, as his board repeatedly urged him to do. Fortunately for Ivester, in this country, in this millennium, failed leaders get golden parachutes. They aren't struck down in the public square. His successor, Doug Daft, observed that the company had bungled its European alliances because it had on American blinders when it needed global vision. "You've got to be able to look at things through their eyes," Daft said.[8]

In fact, globalization has raised the stakes for leaders everywhere—the context they must grasp is no longer simply an institutional one or even a national one. Instead, today's leaders have to be able to respond nimbly to an avalanche of information from around the world and to grasp multiple contexts, some very different from the ones they grew up in. They can do so only with the help of other eyes, ears, and minds. Without damning his predecessor by name, Daft noted that Ivester ignored an invaluable source of information within the company—the loyal contrarians who disagreed with him. Ivester discouraged dissent, even though, as Daft correctly observed: "You need a network to prevent the danger that people will stop telling you things." Daft added, "I don't just want to hear good news."

The Flawed Logic of Yes-Men at Compaq

Compaq's former CEO Eckhard Pfeiffer shared many of Ivester's faults. He had an A list of executive yes-men and a B list of astute observers willing to speak truth to power, and he ignored the latter right out of a job. Pfeiffer refused the good counsel of those on his staff who realized Gateway and Dell were leaving Compaq in the dust by using the Internet to tailor their products to individual consumers and provide them with customer service in a keystroke. Pfeiffer not only failed to notice that other firms were gaining on his, he also failed to seize the opportunities created by the Internet as others had done. Like Coriolanus, he became isolated, unable or unwilling to reach out to all but a handful of colleagues and cut off from customers and their needs.

Cerner's Obsessive Communication

Every day we see examples of leadership gone awry. One of the most egregious cases in recent memory was that of Neal Patterson, head of the health care information technology firm Cerner. His is an almost textbook case of failure to engage others through shared meaning. Patterson is the CEO who dashed off the following blistering e-mail to his managers: "The parking lot is sparsely used at 8 A.M.; likewise at 5 P.M. As managers, you either do not know what your EMPLOYEES are doing; or YOU do not CARE . . . you have a problem and you will fix it or I will replace you. NEVER in my career have I allowed a team which worked for me to think they had a 40 hour job. I have allowed YOU to create a culture which is permitting this . . . if you are the problem, pack your bags. Folks, this is a management problem, not an EMPLOYEE problem. Congratulations, you are management . . . You have allowed this to get to this state. You have two weeks. Tick, tock."[9]

This is obsessive communication—a leadership skill—made poisonous. Had Patterson not been a founder of the company, the tick-tock he heard might have been the sound of his own tenure ending. It was bad enough that Patterson did the electronic equivalent of screeching at his executives with those contemptuous capital letters. It was bad enough that he patronized his managers and reminded them in the nastiest way possible that he was in charge, not them. Even worse, however, Patterson failed (or as he might have written, FAILED) to remember that in today's corporate world employees are not passive pawns, but intellectual capital. They are not just an asset, they are the asset, and they deserve to be treated well—not just because it the right thing to do, but because it is the only smart and fiscally responsible thing to do. Many things matter in today's highly competitive marketplace, but a full parking lot at seven o'clock in the morning is not one of them. That Patterson actually distributed such an e-mail, whose real message is that Patterson is an authoritarian executive with a tin ear and a blind eye, is the most remarkable aspect of the entire incident. It was the corporate equivalent of a suicide note. Within days, Cerner's stock price slipped 22 percent.

It is interesting to contrast Patterson's self-destructive behavior with that of Michael Klein, in his latest venture as a dot-com executive. Klein knows what Patterson failed or refused to see—that talented employees demand respect if only because they are invaluable. Klein told us he spends much of his time cheerleading in order to retain his essential knowledge workers. It isn't easy and it isn't always fun, Klein made clear, but it must be done. In a General Motors or other traditional business, he said, "Lots of people can walk out. They've still got a manufacturing plant. People go on strike, they'll still own all their assets. If we had a breakdown of key talent walking out the door, we would be lost." The reality that Klein has grasped is that his employees are greatly talented, intelligent, and fully cognizant of how much the company needs them. Moral issues aside, Klein would no more alienate his staff than his grandfather would have damaged his paint-manufacturing equipment. As a result, Klein spends much of his time "playing armchair psychologist and partner and coach." The job requires just as much adaptive capacity as did his more entrepreneurial enterprises. He was obviously surprised when a number of employees complained that the office was not sufficiently "fun." Instead of responding contemptuously, he took the complaint seriously and responded creatively. One result: a $40,000 employee party that featured such hip attractions as a rock-climbing wall and Sumo wrestlers as well as a band.

Creating Shared Meaning

Understanding context is rarely easy, and sometimes even talented leaders are destined to fail. Procter & Gamble has had a reputation for retaining CEOs more patiently than is the current norm in a world where CEO honeymoons tend to be painfully short. Former CEO Durk Jager was a man of considerable vision who saw the need to modernize the tradition-bound consumer-goods giant. Shortly after he took over in 1999, Jager announced a sweeping restructuring that he called Organization 2005. Jager planned nothing less than a cultural revolution for the huge firm. Its four regional business units would be replaced by seven global ones. Much of his plan hinged on getting the entire company, once notorious for its reliance on laboriously vetted one-page memos, wired for instant electronic communication. Fifty-four official change agents, all computer-savvy, were sent out to revolutionize its offices and plants throughout the world.

The result was Jager's precipitous and very public fall. Jager's was a classic fumble. He moved before he was able to get the rest of the company behind his innovative plan for change—before, in the language of our model, he had engaged others by creating shared meaning. Whether the plan was a good one or not, Jager never managed to communicate the urgency and superiority of his new vision for the company. His decision to eliminate 15,000 of the corporation's 110,000 jobs undoubtedly contributed to employee resistance. Employees were further alienated when they discovered that the company had tapped the phones of three staffers suspected of revealing insider information.

Jager also bungled external communications. He allowed the CFO to announce that profits would be up one quarter when they were actually down, triggering a plunge in the stock price. There were other career-ending moves as well. The company has long been dogged by public relations missteps and damaging rumors, the most persistent being the famous urban legend that the Procter & Gamble logo has satanic significance. Along with the embarrassing release of falsely optimistic earnings numbers, the company had another public relations crisis on Jager's watch. It pulled advertising from Dr. Laura Schlessinger's controversial radio and TV programs because of her antigay stance, then was hit with a backlash from conservative consumers who thought the company's online apologia was too pro-gay. If all of P & G had been behind Jager, he might have weathered these brouhahas. But with the stock price down and the company getting unflattering media coverage, Jager was booted after only seventeen months in charge. In fact, many of the changes Jager made have stuck, including streamlining the product-development process (its innovative mop, the Swiffer, was brought to market in just eighteen months) and converting the company to instant communication worldwide. But Jager did not survive the turmoil he unleashed, in large part because he was unable to galvanize and inspire others. "In hindsight, it's clear we changed too much too fast," his successor, A. G. Lafley, told the press. Had Jager found a way to engage others, he might well have been hailed as a corporate hero.

Warnaco's Linda Wachner is an even more dramatic example of someone with vision who failed to engage others through shared meaning. Like Patterson, she was fatally deficient in emotional intelligence, particularly empathy. As one observer told the *New York Times* in 2000, as the company struggled to avoid bankruptcy: "She is the main reason why Warnaco has grown and the main reason it has fallen apart. There is some genius there, but she cannot run a $2 billion corporation by herself."[10]

No one can. Success can create enormous arrogance, especially when coupled with emotional tone-deafness. During Wachner's fifteen years as CEO (she was finally fired in 2001), she seemed to be increasingly insensitive to the contribution others made to the enterprise and to their feelings. According to the *Times,* she "developed a reputation for demoralizing employees by publicly dressing them down for missing sales and profit goals or for simply displeasing her. Often, many former employees said, the attacks were personal rather than professional." Former employees also reported that she used crude and racist language, a charge she denied. If true, however, that is the kind of insensitivity to cultural change—to put the kindest possible spin on it—that sinks executives, however talented in other ways (a dozen fallen bigwigs in professional sports come to mind). Such insensitivity represents not only a moral failure but also a colossal failure to understand context.

As a female leader, Wachner may have borne more burdens than her male counterparts, including being held to a higher standard, but she did seem to have an unusual propensity for undermining herself at every turn. Leaders of troubled corporations such as Warnaco cannot hope to reverse negative momentum by themselves. They must find ways to inspire and mobilize others in the organization in order to survive. Wachner struggled doggedly to keep her company alive, but, in the course of those struggles, she never managed to learn the essential lessons or acquire the necessary skills that would have equipped her for the next round of challenges—skills that our geeks and geezers have in abundance.

Every leader is a work in progress, however. Time will tell if Wachner's spectacular failure will prove to be the crucible in which she receives the priceless education that will equip her for successes in the future. William Butler Yeats wrote a marvelous little poem "To a Friend Whose Work Has Come to Nothing":

> *Now all the truth is out, . . .*
> *Be secret and exult,*
> *Because of all things known*
> *That is most difficult.*[11]

Failure is hard, yes, but instructive as well. If failed leaders are wise, and have developed the requisite adaptive capacity, they will look dispassionately at what went wrong and exploit that hard-won knowledge at the next opportunity. As Sidney Harman said: "The whole point of failure is to learn from it."

Having a vision and being able to sell it is an essential task of leadership. To a person, our geezers have become adept at galvanizing whatever organization they lead. They are able and obsessive communicators. Bob Crandall, former CEO of American Airlines, told us: "You simply cannot lead if you cannot tell the other guy what it is you want and expect." And, he added: "If you can't rouse the crowd, you cannot lead effectively." Business visionary Dee Hock, who founded Visa International, observed: "When you induce behavior, that's essential to leadership." Just as writers must find their voice, so leaders must find an individual and persuasive voice, an authentic version of themselves that engages and recruits others. As longtime Girl Scouts of America CEO Frances Hesselbein observed, "You lead by voice."

Leaders, Followers, and a Common Goal

Stripped to its essentials, leadership involves just three things—a leader, followers, and a common goal. Despite the relative inexperience of our geeks, many already know that their first and, in many ways, most important task is articulating their vision and making it their followers' own. Cofounder Young Shin says of his colleagues at Embark.com: "A lot of leading these people . . . is having them buy into the vision." Dan Cunningham, founder and CEO, or "Chief Chokolada," of Dan's Chocolates, uses the term "revolutionizing" to describe the process whereby he recruits employees to his vision. Teach For America's Wendy Kopp believes: "The essence of leadership is mobilizing people to achieve great things."

Effective leaders don't just impose their vision on others, they recruit others to a shared vision. Especially in our digital age, when power tends to coalesce around ideas, not position, leadership is a partnership, not a sinecure. Former military nurse Lingyun Shao told us that she believes "the essence of leadership is taking care of your subordinates." And she makes clear that she does not see this as a paternalistic relationship. Rather, she sees the leader as a steward, even a servant: "When you're a leader," she says, "you have to remember that you work for them, not the other way around." That advice applies in many settings, as Arthur Levitt describes in the sidebar that follows.

A RTHUR LEVITT, 70-year-old former head of the Securities and Exchange Commission, told us of a lesson he learned about engaging others through shared meaning from Senator Phil Gramm:

> When I came here, first thing I learned from my predecessor was he was not popular with the staff. He was very autocratic. And very formal and could be very nasty. So instead of spending my time with the Congress, instead of spending my time with the business community, I spent my time with the staff. At my own expense I had bagel parties for divisions, and I talked to them and I listened to them and I'd hear their complaints and I'd reach out to them.
>
> One act struck me as the most extraordinary since I've been here, dealing with a regal group of individuals who represent the Congress and the Senate of the United States, where you have to just kiss their ass morning, day, and night. It involved Phil Gramm. Phil Gramm had proposed a financial restructuring bill that was very important to him and to the country, and at one point in the negotiations where he wanted our support, I called him at six o'clock at night and said there were aspects of the bill I couldn't go along with. He said, "Where are you?" I said, "In my office." He said, "I'll be right over." And he came over himself.
>
> I learned a lesson there and I'm lusting for the opportunity to do the same thing in one of life's situations where it is most unlikely that I have to go to someone's office. That's just what I will do.

Sky Dayton shares the view that leaders must trust and empower followers, one way that leaders create shared meaning. "A very important part of leadership is the ability to trust other people and to hand them the reins and let them drive," Dayton says. When we pressed him to elaborate on that credo, he told us the following story, about returning from a ski trip with a candidate to succeed him as CEO of Earthlink:

> *I had this car with big wide wheels that wouldn't take snow chains. We had to drive back on these really icy, snowy roads. And I never experienced driving in snow before, but he did, because he was from the East Coast. . . . So he talked me down the mountain. At one point I remember we did a whole 360 as we were driving. But he was really cool about it the whole way. And I don't know, we just clicked. There was something about that. I knew we were going to be in some pretty tough situations in the years ahead, and he was pretty cool under pressure.*

Dayton was able to abandon his ego in order to unleash the talents of others, an important aspect of emotional intelligence. Moreover, he was able to craft a parable-like story around the event, one that vividly communicates his trust in his subordinates. It is a story that he can tell the people who work for and around him. And it has probably already become part of what management theorist Edgar Schein calls "the founder's tale"—the resonant, community-building stories that lie at the heart of so many vigorous organizational cultures.

Doing It Right

While we can learn a great deal from failure, it is even more illuminating to study exemplary leaders doing it right. Born in 1929, Frank Gehry has emerged in recent years as the most influential architect of the past half-century. His unique postmodern style combines technical virtuosity with a personal vision that results in buildings that float and undulate and make viewers fall hopelessly in love. "Frozen jazz," an admirer called Gehry's work. His Guggenheim Museum in Bilbao, Spain, is a unique phenomenon in the architecture of the last thirty years, drawing millions from around the world to an otherwise drab industrial town to see a structure, rather than a collection. Gehry is the only artist one associates with Bilbao. Although he has only 130 people working under him in his Santa Monica office, Gehry is a leader of the first order, a major shaper of the visual culture of our time.

Gehry exemplifies all four of the essential competencies of leadership. His adaptive capacity was evident as a teenager. At 18 he left his native Toronto for Los Angeles, a city rarely thought of as an architectural mecca. Gehry liked that. As a first-class noticer, he realized that a city without a Chartres or other architectural icon was an empty canvas on which he could express himself. Cities like Toronto were not the future. They were centralized and authoritarian. Los Angeles was a huge pinball machine, a diverse jumble that energized him. Los Angeles was opportunity. "There was a great freedom in Los Angeles, because there wasn't the infrastructure like in Toronto, the European cities, or even New York," he says. "This was the Wild West. . . . And maybe this is wishful thinking, but it represents democracy to me."

When you design structures as unprecedented as Gehry's, you must be able to engage others through shared meaning or the projects will never be built. Gehry will accept a commission only if the ultimate decision makers are actively involved in the process. As he puts it, "I need Michael Eisner to play with me to do a building for him." Gehry does this for practical reasons, not ideo-logical ones: "I insist on those relationships because the buildings look strange, and you've got to get into the logic system of why they are there. . . . Once you've been working with me and develop a relationship to whatever logic I bring to the project, then you realize it's not so from left field." When clients are engaged and share his vision for a project, he says, "They're in it, they get it." He gives the example of his most famous project to date. "Take Bilbao," he says. "Everybody gets Bilbao now. But you try to explain that up front. Whoa. Nobody got it."

Nobody except his clients. Gehry was able to explain the logic of the fluid titanium structure in ways that not only sold them on it, but gave them a sense of ownership. "They believed," he says.

"The client group I worked with really believed that I could do it. And they supported it and they listened and I didn't sell them a pig in a poke." When Gehry can't create that kind of consensus, he walks away. He decided not to build a new home for the *New York Times* because he did not share the agendas of the commercial partners—even though he says the design was the best he has ever done.

Gehry also encourages dissent, another attribute of those who successfully engage others in a shared vision. Even the most junior members of Gehry's team, he says, "know that I'm not tender. They can talk about what they don't like." He says that "the senior guys" in the firm also tell him when an idea is over the top or not technically feasible. "I usually know I can't go there, but I test the waters a lot," he says. "Having them as the gatekeeper means that I can soar a little bit, and they'll pull me back. So I feel comfortable that they won't let me get out into outer space." Imagine how invested in the firm such partners are, how Gehry's willingness to hear them out both reflects genuine respect for them and helps cement their loyalty to the enterprise.

Voice and Character

Voice may seem an odd term to use in connection with Gehry, who works in a visual medium, but he clearly has a distinctive, confident one. He is obviously self-aware (a component of emotional intelligence), and says he learned more about himself and how he relates to other people as a result of group therapy. "As soon as I started listening to them and not sitting in judgment or sitting pissed off . . . and thinking they were wasting my time, it just changed," he says of his group experience. "I started listening and found myself involved with their lives and they became involved with mine."

A strong set of values and rules of conduct were common to all our leaders, independent of their theology, and Gehry is no exception. Unlike many architects, who have unpaid interns and other workers, Gehry insists on paying everyone on his staff. This was true even when he was starting out. From the beginning, he refused to do projects for free, as many architects do when trying to establish themselves. He told potential clients: "I'll only do it if I get paid because I can't do it without the help of people, and I'm not going to use people." He evidences the same sort of principles in his dealings with clients. We asked one of his former clients if, as Gehry says, he completes projects on time, on or under budget, and with the full partnership of his client. "Yes and yes and yes," the former client, a college president, replied.

Leadership is always about character, a formidable and protean word with twenty-six definitions in the *American Heritage Dictionary* (Fourth Edition). Our favorite comes from William James, who famously wrote, "I have often thought that the best way to define a man's character would be to seek out the particular mental or moral attitude in which, when it came upon him, he felt himself most deeply and intensively active and alive. At such moments, there is a voice inside which speaks and says, 'This is the real me.' "[12] Sometimes, as the following sidebar demonstrates, that voice can bring reason to a much larger audience.

What people respond to in leaders such as Gehry is not any espoused religion or philosophy, but their conviction, their powerful sense of justice, and their passionate desire to do the right thing. Our leaders include Protestants, Catholics, Jews, and atheists. Whatever they believe, they behave in ways that reflect their awareness of the value and rights of other people: None lives in a universe in which he or she is the sun. Like it or not, we are all post-Copernican. We know that millions of people have followed charismatic but evil men—that is the great tragedy of the twentieth century. But under normal circumstances, people prefer to give their allegiance to leaders of integrity. People know in their bones, or even their genes, it is the right thing to do.

A few of our leaders say that their lives are guided by a specific religious faith. John Gardner said his work was underpinned by his Protestant faith. Father Robert J. Drinan says: "For a convinced Catholic, he or she has a bedrock of convictions that bring

J ACK COLEMAN, 78-year-old former president of Haverford College, recalled a day etched in memory in which his values and his abilities as a leader were put to the test:

There's one moment in my Haverford career that people talk about more than any other. It's because of the Quaker influence where there's very heavy emphasis on nonviolence. It's part of the tenet of the college and accepted by everybody there. And at one point when the Vietnam war was going particularly badly, the bombings at Cambodia and the killings at Kent State had taken place, word got to me that after our Tuesday morning collection, which is a gathering of all the students, a group of those most avidly working for peace led by a rather radical faculty member, were going to pull down the American flag and burn it. Word also got to me that we still had the survivors of what had once been our football team, a team now gone, and they were darn sure that wasn't going to happen at all. They were going to make sure it didn't. And any one of those football players could have taken on three of the peaceniks and handled it very nicely. And I knew this when I was sitting in collection, that this was going to happen. And absolutely baffled. What do you do about that? The possibility of violence, the flag being burned . . . [Coleman stopped for a moment]. I walked out at the end of the collection and there was a substantial gathering around the flagpole. I saw both factions there. And somewhere up above maybe, from somewhere a voice came to me, gave me a message. And I went to the peace faction and said, "Instead of burning the flag, why not get a bucket of Tide and soap and water? Wash the flag and put it back up." That's what happened. The troops dispersed. I don't know where that message came from, why. Certainly I didn't have it while I was sitting in [collection], but leadership there was luck I guess. That message came along. It was a wonderful moment.

peace and tranquility and direction in your life. And I think that when I deal with people, they understand that . . . I'm not seeking to impose it on them, but I have a whole range of bedrock convictions from which I can operate." Sky Dayton believes his training as a Scientologist set him on a moral path that includes the desire "to have a positive impact on the world."

We suspect that the religious practices of our leaders are largely irrelevant to those who follow them. The trust that Sidney Harman's factory workers put in him was not because of his religious beliefs, but because of his obvious personal integrity, the respect he showed them and his willingness to put his money into projects like piano lessons that enhanced their quality of life. Former Haverford president Jack Coleman is admired, not because he is a member of the Society of Friends, but because of his willingness to walk in other people's shoes by working as a trash collector and living on the streets. Ed Guthman's Judaism may be of private importance to him, but it is his commitment to social justice that is relevant to his leadership. Whether Sidney Rittenberg was a Marxist or a Schumpeterian, he was concerned with every person's right to a full belly and freedom from fear. He has always practiced a kind of rational virtuousness in the cause of human betterment. Some of our leaders followed their moral compasses in directions their faiths of record would never have taken them. Former nun Elizabeth McCormack was on the board of Planned Parenthood even though she knew it might result in her excommunication. She was convinced that it was the right thing to do.

Some of our leaders have made tough moral choices that their followers probably know nothing about but that contribute to their moral authority. An example is supercoach John Wooden, who, early in his career, refused to participate in a national tournament that denied equal access to his black players.

A number of our leaders credited family members with their moral educations. Nonviolence activist Lorig Charkoudian told us that her grandparents were survivors of the Armenian genocide. "That shaped my view of the world and decisions about what I needed to do in the world," she explains. "There was a lot of hatred [in the world] and there was a lot of pain, and all that had to be responded to." Dan Cunningham's moral inspiration was the steadfast refusal of his physician father to accept rewards from drug companies for prescribing their products. Cunningham recalls that his father always focused on what was best for his patients. "It was clear that money was not the motivating factor behind his work," Cunningham says. The lesson conveyed by both his parents: "The idea is basically what you can do for others and the community, and that's where your first thought should be."

The Integrity Tripod

Finally, let us turn to the fourth competence of leaders: integrity. We have to plead guilty to the charge that we've been using lots of words that are loosely related to integrity, and are more or less interchangeable; words and phrases such as moral compass, moral code, codes of conduct, values, ethics, character, voice, ideals, beliefs, ideology, principles, philosophy, and so forth. Many of these words were put into play in the preceding section, Voice and Character, and while they have some rough equivalence to integrity, we have to give integrity a more precise meaning. (We were even tempted to coin a neologism, "integritous," because that would be a convenient and shorthand way to describe all of our geeks and geezers. Fortunately, our aesthetic sensibilities prevailed and we dropped that vagrant thought.) It is high time we returned to the "I" word with a hope to refine its meaning.

The integrity of leaders is composed of three elements: ambition, competence, and moral compass. Think of these three as legs of a tripod that have to be kept in balance. By ambition, we mean the desire to achieve something, whether for personal gain or the good of the community or both. Competence includes expertise and mastery of specific skills. Moral compass comprises virtues that acknowledge the individual's membership in the larger human community as well as the capacity to distinguish between good and evil. In decent leaders, instead of merely successful ones, all three elements are in balance, forming a kind of tripod. But when any single element dominates the leader's behavior and the tripod becomes too wobbly, he or she is at risk of lacking integrity. Take ambition. Without it, there is no vision or engine for change. But unbridled ambition produces the worst sort of demagoguery. Ian McKellen's rendition of Richard III, bedecked with Nazi swastikas and a faux moustache, reminds us not only of Hitler and his scheme of world conquest, but of a danger that predated Hitler and survives him: the danger of giving power to people who can't live without it.

But it's not only in the political world that we see ambition run amok. Think of J. Albert Dunlap, who fudged his credentials and outright lied in order to advance his career. Long before the full extent of "Chainsaw Al's" dishonesty became public, some observers were appalled at his behavior and how he was widely lauded despite his ruthlessness. CEO David Friedson, of Sunbeam rival Windmere-Durable Holdings, described Dunlap as an individual with "no values, no honor, no loyalty, and no ethics. And yet he was held up as a corporate god in our culture. It greatly bothered me." With hindsight, we can see ethical lapses all along the road that make Dunlap's fall seem almost inevitable. The more recent and far more egregious collapse of Enron's ethically challenged leadership, accompanied by its Arthur Andersen "auditors," makes the Dunlap moral lapse look like small beer. Let's not mince words. Ambition, absent a moral compass, is naked destructiveness.

Let's turn to competence. If competence becomes mere virtuosity, it too can become monstrous. Many of the technocrats of e-business are examples of individuals whose leadership is undermined by their overreliance on technology and their failure to develop all the important skills unrelated to their beloved machines. At their worst, they become number-crunching, green-eye-shaded, statistical Vulcans, unable to respond to the many nontechnological needs of their organizations. Even during Harold Geneen's glory days at ITT, his leadership was undermined by a preternatural obsession with information, facts, numbers, charts, and all manner of technological fixes.

This is an extremely complicated issue and one not to be avoided or finessed, because it exposes the genius and the contradiction of our most successful human institutions, those wondrous behemoths Max Weber immortalized with the word "bureaucracy." The genius is what Weber characterized as their rationality. The contradiction is one that C. Wright Mills pointed out many years ago, the tension between rationality and reason.[13]

It is illuminating to examine that tension refracted through the prism of the recent GE/EPA controversy about dredging the Hudson River in order to clean up the PCBs dumped by a GE subsidiary over the course of many years. Jack Welch, one of the most celebrated CEOs of our time and one whom we personally admire, steadfastly opposed what he considered a stupid ruling by the EPA. From what we know of the case, he's probably right. GE's resistance to further perturbing the river's sediment was not at all irrational. But what GE's rational, cost/benefit analysis failed to take into account was the appropriate degree of sensitivity to the surrounding communities, to the environmentalists, and to the long and costly litigation, as well as the extremely negative PR problem GE's obstinately "right" decision would and did cost. The decision to contest the case was obviously rational. But was it reasonable? As our human institutions become more rationalized, leaders must be vigilantly aware of how technical/rational virtuosity, absent a moral compass (in the GE case being tone deaf to their noncorporate stakeholders), can lead to what Mills referred to as "crackpot rationality."

Whatever else a leader must do, he or she must know where to draw the line and find a way to keep these three elements—ambition, technical competence, and moral compass—in balance. One of the dangers of giddy immersion in a task characterizes many great organizations and their leaders—the lack of time for reflection on moral and ethical issues. It was only at the very end of the Manhattan Project, for example, after the bomb was close to completion, that some of the scientists stepped back from the technological race that obsessed them to consider the moral implications of what they were doing. The result was the realization by Niels Bohr and others that nuclear proliferation would be a human disaster, and steps had to be taken to prevent it. But that was well after the fact, because the smart group of gifted scientists, gathered around J. Robert Oppenheimer, simply couldn't resist the enormous challenge of building the bomb. It was irresistible catnip to them because, as Oppenheimer said when he agreed to lead the project, "It was too sweet a problem."[14]

We've talked about unbridled ambition and gifted competence absent a moral compass; what about moral compass absent ambition or competence? That's a more difficult and complex question and could deceive one to think it's of less consequence than the other two. After all, how many examples come to mind of individuals who have a powerful moral compass without competence and ambition? When we ask our students and friends this question, they often and incorrectly come up with names such as Jimmy Carter or Mother Theresa. Mother Theresa's competence and ambition were monumental, and whatever one thinks of Carter's success as president, he certainly had enough ambition and competence. The only clear example that comes quickly to mind is the enigmatic Shakespearean character, Hamlet. A strong moral compass, to be sure: to take sweet revenge on the killer of his father. He was highly principled but feckless, thrusting his sword in all the wrong places and killing off the innocents as well as the indifferent in equal numbers.

As we think about this question more, however, we do find such characters in real life, the likes of Father Charles Coughlin and Huey Long, who with their charismatic appeal and seductive ideas can trap people in false dreams and fatal folly. A strong moral compass, without competence or accountability, can be as dangerous as ambition without a moral compass. Such leaders can become, at their harmless best, objects of enchantment or, at worst, venomous pied pipers.

But let us return to our original task for this section, to refine the meaning of the word *integrity*. The word has taken on so many different connotations, has been casually finessed or used in so many disparate ways, that it helps to add one more critical distinction before we can move on: the difference between voice and character, which we discussed in the preceding section, and the key concept of this section, integrity.

Historian Arthur Schlesinger, Jr., once said that six individuals shaped the destiny of the twentieth century: Lenin, Hitler, Stalin, Roosevelt, Churchill, and Mao. All undeniably profoundly influential leaders. All certainly had clear, resonant, and strong voices. William James, using his own definition, would certainly have called them men of character.[15] Voice and character, big time, no question. We will argue that all were authentic and "real." They were all zealous believers in their ultimate goals. For example, Hitler's obsession with anti-Semitism wasn't just an act or a political move. It was a major aspect of his belief system. All these individuals had a reasonable degree of emotional intelligence. To call them "obsessive communicators" is an understatement. None of them lacked self-confidence. In fact, all six of these twentieth-century giants not only possessed all the major factors of voice that all our geeks and geezers embodied, but voice was indispensable for their success as leaders. But we now know, looking back through the shining ether of time, that four of the six (Lenin, Stalin, Hitler, and Mao), were responsible for the murder of some 80 million innocent souls. (Some twentieth-century historians put the figure closer to 120 million.) Their tripod of integrity was missing one leg, a moral compass. Integrity, in the most common dictionary usage, means wholeness and completeness. In their skewed vision of reality, their voices of evil were uncommonly effective and monstrously influential. All they lacked was the wholeness of integrity.

Although leaders rarely talk about it, those we most admire, from Abraham Lincoln to Nelson Mandela, have managed to keep the three legs of the integrity tripod in balance. Although most of our geeks have yet to have their integrity tested, it was heartening to see how important the whole issue of balance is to them. As a result, they may be better prepared than their elders were to keep one aspect of their lives from taking over.

At the outset of this chapter, we referred to the "Big Four" qualities of leadership: adaptive capacity, engaging others through shared meaning, a distinctive voice, and integrity. None of these four is especially new or unfamiliar to a reader versed in the literature on leadership. To a greater or lesser extent, they've been part of the leadership canon, but always singly. They've never been considered as a quartet of interrelated factors based on a theory of human development. This is the most thrilling discovery we made as we studied our geeks and geezers: that the factors that allow an individual to lead for a lifetime are indeed identical to the qualities of adult learning discussed in the previous chapter on crucibles. Moreover, they are the same factors that make a person a healthy, fully integrated human being.

Wonder and Neoteny

Inevitably, when we look at our geezers, we are struck anew by their capacity for wonder and other evidence of neoteny. A friend with whom we discussed our study suggested that the octogenarian zest that many of our older leaders radiate is the result of denial. Not at all. Our geezers were able to assess their abilities and limitations quite realistically. Indeed, at age 85 and again at age 90, urban activist Walter Sondheim wrote letters to respected friends imploring them to alert him to any evidence of diminished capacity. "The older you get, the less people are willing to tell you that your competence has begun to slip and it's time to hang it up," Sondheim explains. "And I was terribly afraid of [that], and I wanted each of them to have the opportunity to write me a letter and make it anonymous."

While our geezers do not deny their aging, they refuse to be defined by it. Each of them has a sense of being ripe with hard-won insight and ability and, at the same time, is eager for the next adventure. They are ready, as creative people always are, to leap into the unknown. A memorable passage from Henry James, written in midlife, expresses the eagerness we saw in our geezers: "I am in full possession of accumulated resources," he wrote. "I have only to use them, to insist, to persist, to do something more. . . . The way to do it—to affirm one's self *sur la fin*—is to strike as many notes, deep, full and rapid, as one can. All life is—at my age, with all one's artistic soul the record of it—in one's pocket, as it were. Go on, my boy, and strike hard. . . . Try everything, do everything, render everything—be an artist, be distinguished to the last."[16]

This is essentially the mantra of Tennyson's Ulysses, the sure and certain belief that "though much is taken, much abides" and the confidence that "some work of noble note may yet be done." Like Ulysses, every one of our geezers has "a hungry heart." They are focused on the future, not the past, and as addicted to life, as energized by it, as they ever were.

That is neoteny. We use the term, of course, as a metaphor, but let's look again at the scientific principle of neoteny. The retention of youthful characteristics in adulthood, neoteny is an evolutionary engine. It is the winning, puppyish quality of certain ancient wolves that allowed them to evolve into dogs. Over thousands of years, humans favored those wolves that were the friendliest, the most approachable, the most curious, the least likely to attack without warning, the ones that readily locked eyes with humans and seemed almost human in their eager response to people; the ones, in short, that stayed the most like puppies.

Neoteny's Power to Recruit

Recently, scientists studying perception have found that certain physical characteristics and qualities elicit a nurturing response in human adults. Those characteristics and behaviors are those evidenced by human infants—and by puppies. Babies have relatively large eyes that will lock onto those of adults without fear. Infants have relatively large foreheads and flat, nonprominent features except for those big eyes. When infants see an adult, they will often respond with a smile, a smile that begins small and grows slowly into a radiant grin that makes the adult feel that he or she is the center of the universe or, as they say in the South, "hangs the moon." Recent studies of bonding indicate that nursing and other intimate interactions with the infant cause the mother's system to be flooded with oxytocin, a calming, feel-good hormone that is a powerful antidote to cortisol, the hormone produced by stress. Oxytocin appears to be the glue that produces bonding. And the baby's distinctive look and behaviors are what causes oxytocin to be released in the fortunate adult. That appearance— the one that pulls an involuntary "aaah" out of us whenever we see a baby—and those oxytocin-inducing behaviors allow infants to recruit adults to be their nurturers, essential if such vulnerable and incompletely developed creatures are to survive.

The power of neoteny to recruit protectors and nurturers was vividly illustrated recently in the former Soviet Union. Forty years ago a Soviet scientist decided to start breeding silver foxes for neoteny at a Siberian fur farm. The goal was to create a new, tamer fox that would go with less fuss to slaughter than the typical silver fox. Only the least aggressive, most approachable animals were bred. The experiment continued for forty years, and today, after thirty-five generations, the farm is home to a new breed of tame foxes that look and act more like juvenile foxes and even dogs than like their wild forebears. The physical changes in the animals are remarkable (some have floppy, dog-like ears), but what is truly stunning is the change neoteny has wrought in the human response to them. Instead of taking advantage of the fact that these neotenic animals don't snap and snarl on the way to their deaths, their human keepers appear to have been recruited by their newly cute and endearing charges. The keepers and the foxes appear to have formed close bonds, so close that the keepers are trying to find ways to save the animals from slaughter.

A similar process may explain the form of bonding we call mentoring, a crucible common to so many leaders. The mentor sees in the prospective protégé a youthful energy and enthusiasm—we are tempted to call it "wide-eyed enthusiasm," to bolster the point—that triggers some primal desire to nurture, teach, and protect. However the mentor justifies his or her readiness to lavish time and other resources on the mentored (a desire to give back to the community; "she reminds me of myself at that age"), the real reason for the mentor's devotion may be as old as time and as inescapable as chemistry. It may be that the mentor benefits physiologically, in increased levels of oxytocin, just as he or she surely benefits socially, from camaraderie and from the opportunity to learn the often difficult-to-access realities of a generation younger than one's own. And there may be evolutionary benefits as well—a close relationship with a younger person may be advantageous to an aging individual whose strength and other physical powers are on the wane. There may even be an evolutionary pay-off for the mentor in that he or she is being coached in neoteny, that most precious and life-enhancing of qualities, whether either party knows it or not.

It's worth remembering where the word *mentor* comes from. Mentor is the trusted friend Odysseus enlists to look after his son Telemachus when the hero sets out on his long journey. Created by Athena, Mentor embodies the wisdom of both genders. Transferring wisdom from one generation to another is central to the notion of mentoring. But these are always reciprocal relationships. There is a wonderful circularity about the mentoring process, whether it is the one Homer describes or such real-life examples as that of Helen Keller and Annie Sullivan. We all know that Sullivan was the gifted teacher who unlocked the intelligence of young, blind, and deaf Helen Keller. Less well known is that Keller taught her beloved teacher Braille when Sullivan finally lost her limited sight.

We suspect that what we call charisma—that never adequately defined quality that makes slavering devotees of us all—is actually neoteny. Charisma has the same essential element of recruitment, which so well serves the charismatic individual. The adored one receives not only adulation but countless other intangible benefits as well. Among these Matthew effects (a reference to the assurance in the Gospel According to Matthew that the rich get richer) are nonstop stimulation (so conducive to continued learning) and a dependable, external prop to self-esteem.

Whether it subsumes charisma or not, neoteny is a treasure. We are convinced it is the great secret shared by our geezers—the X factor that allows them to continue leading, learning, and feeling well, whatever their physical health.

Forever Young

As we said earlier, neoteny is a metaphor for all the youthful gifts the luckiest of us never lose. One of the Grant study men was asked what he had gotten out of his successful psychoanalysis. He answered that he had stopped biting his fingernails. And, he said: "I am more like I was at four than at seven." A good case can be made for nurturing your inner four-year-old. As Vaillant writes: "From four to five we are all romantics; we are all embryonic royalty, budding ballerinas, or intrepid astronauts; we are all fearless, open, affectionate, and beautiful."[17] Time, the loss of friends and loved ones, and a society that is often cruel in its denial of the worth of the old can take a terrible toll. But the person who remains a four-year-old—at least who retains the best qualities of one—has little time for mourning what is lost. In the now decidedly dated language of the human potential movement, four-year-olds live in the now. They also live outside themselves and in relation to other people. They do not spend a great deal of time in self-conscious contemplation. They have trouble to get into, trees to climb, frogs to find, mud pies to fashion. They have things to do. That quality of utter engagement with the world is as attractive in an 80-year-old as in a preschooler.

Neotenic Max Klein knew instinctively that he had things to learn from his grandson as well as to teach. In the course of our interviews, one leader told a wonderful story about writer Norman Corwin, whose 100-year-old father would call him every day and say, "Norman, are you keeping your mind active?" Neotenics keep their minds active as a matter of course. Our neotenic geezers tend to use their bodies with youthful brio as well. Near-octogenarian Bob Galvin windsurfs and takes pride in teaching the sport to others, including Sony founder Akio Morita. Former Securities and Exchange Commission chairman Arthur Levitt, Jr., likes to trek with Outward Bound. Frank Gehry and former Los Angeles mayor Richard Riordan play cutthroat ice hockey on local teams. A half-dozen of our geezers are enthusiastic tennis players, regularly defeating younger spouses. Bette Davis once famously said, "Old age is no place for sissies." Old age is one of the most predictable of crucibles, and eventually many of our most active geezers may have to put down their tennis rackets and find less physically demanding ways to test themselves. But adapting is what our leaders are all about—that, and discovering the best, most meaningful way to live now. Geeks and geezers alike, they still wake up every morning and fall in love with the world all over again.

SIX

A Passion for the Promises of Life

IN DESCRIBING geeks and geezers and their crucibles, we have often discussed mentoring, and a mentor can teach no greater lesson than the centrality of nonstop learning to leading a good and happy life. This is the key lesson that Merlyn teaches the prince who becomes King Arthur in T. H. White's *The Once and Future King*. The magician who is young Arthur's infinitely wise mentor advises the prince that learning is life's only dependable anodyne. "The best thing for being sad is to learn something," Merlyn counsels. "That is the only thing that never fails, the only thing which the mind can never exhaust, never alienate, never be tortured by, never fear or distrust and never dream of regretting."[1]

As we analyzed our findings once again in the final stages of writing this book, we were struck anew by what superb mentors our geeks and geezers are. Like Merlyn, they have powerful lessons to teach and they offer important auguries for the future. We will discuss some of the most important ones—including the implications of our findings for individual, organizational, and social action—later in this chapter. But before we do, let's look back at what we've discovered.

Era-Based Differences

If we had a preconception going into the study, it was that there would be vast differences—in character, style, and aspirations—between the leaders who emerged from the harsh university of World War II and those men and women who created leadership roles for themselves in the now-tattered New Economy. So we were not surprised to discover, in the course of our interviews, that era leaves its imprint on an entire generation, who tend to share everything from worldviews to common taste in footwear. Ultimately, we found a handful of pronounced era-related differences between our geeks and geezers. When our geezers were between the ages of 25 and 30, almost all were focused on finding a secure place for themselves in the world of work. What they desired most was a good job that would allow them to support their families, with an organization where they could stay until retirement. Most of our geezers saw a conventional career path and followed it for a time, if not forever. For the most part, our geeks saw no such clear-cut career path ahead of them. The perceived routes to their destinies were more like highway interchanges designed by Salvador Dali, previously untraveled roads without maps, whose conditions were largely unknown. Our geeks tended to see their careers as acts of the imagination, adventures that they fashioned for themselves—usually in collaboration with their peers—and that they were willing to abandon for another adventure if the current one failed.

Another major difference involved balancing personal life and work. Perhaps because most of our geezers were men, whose wives had made sure their private lives ran efficiently, our geezers said that balance had not been a major concern at mid-career. Most were workaholics, and proud of it. But balancing work and nonwork was an obsession for our geeks. They were clearly torn between ambition and the desire for a fulfilling personal and even spiritual life. Those with young children were doubly torn. Clearly, this difference was the result, at least in part, of an enormous societal change. Around 1970, in the United States, women who had long been marginalized in professional life fought for and won a place at the table. True equity has yet to be achieved, as any working mother racing to get to the day care center before it closes will tell you. But women are now in the game and even shaping its rules and goals. If only because our geeks are more confident than an earlier generation was of meeting their survival needs, they are not content to work to the exclusion of everything else. This was true even when they held self-created jobs in work-places with video games, trampolines, espresso machines, and other fun amenities—perks that disappeared the minute the New Economy began to sour.

One other notable difference emerged. When we queried our geeks and geezers about their heroes, we got very different answers. Our geezers cited world leaders of acknowledged stature such as FDR and Churchill, while our geeks often named a much-loved and admired parent or other relative. Their indifference to heroic leaders of the past reinforced our belief that the Great Man or Woman is dead, and that organizations are increasingly understood to be something more collegial than the lengthened shadows of any individual. As a result, we began to think of our geeks, for the most part, as people without heroes. As Elizabeth Kao explained, she and her fellow geeks are "latchkey kids, a product of divorce, a product of a political system that is in the muck. . . . We don't do this kind of Camelot worship. I don't think that my generation believes that there is a Camelot. There is no ideal place that we can create. There is no utopia."

But that picture changed in an instant on September 11, 2001. In the wake of the terrorist attacks, a national culture that seemed to have lost its ability to distinguish between a hero and a celebrity was transformed. A nation without heroes suddenly had thousands of them. Many were called firefighters. It is impossible to say how long the new reality will last but, in the United States and much of Europe, there is renewed faith in the relevance of heroism and a new longing for leaders of heroic stature. Emblematic of the change: In the same post-attack issue that chronicled the many loves of Madonna, *People* magazine ran a profile of Winston Churchill, whose eloquent ability to engage a nation through shared meaning had become relevant once again.

Commonalities as Well as Differences

Even as we catalogued the era-based differences between generations, we were struck by the even more intriguing similarities. Both generations were able to thrive in complex, ambiguous situations (*messiness,* we called it), sometimes actually seeking out challenging disorder. But voluntary complexity is much easier to bear than the kind that comes roaring out of nowhere. Our geeks, who came of age during an era of relentlessly accelerating change, now face new tests of just how nimble and unflappable they are, given the lingering downturn in the information economy. When our geezers were younger, they tended to seek out fluid, unpredictable situations only after they had experienced the professional and economic stability so highly prized after the Depression and World War II. Having enjoyed the predictable but genuine pleasures of conventional success, many of our geezers became serial risk-takers, distinguishable from our entrepreneurial geeks only by the greater length of the elders' resumes.

There were other important commonalities as well. Whatever his or her generation, each of our leaders was the author, and critic, of his or her own life. In the course of our interviews, it became clear that each person had crafted a resonant story out of the important events and relationships in his or her life. These stories were rarely self-adulatory, but each was a variant on the hero's journey, a tale in which the individual was tested—sometimes sorely—and ultimately triumphed. The trophy was typically a life-changing discovery about the world, the self, or both.

To a person, our leaders felt that the insights they had won justified whatever hardships they had endured. In every case, they learned and they grew. Their stories explained, amused, engaged, and often enrolled others in the narrator's vision. Whatever course their lives had taken, they felt that they had been active participants in, if not captains of, their fate. Many expressed sadness at personal losses, but none expressed regrets.

From the first, our goal was to discover how leadership develops and how it is sustained. Again and again, we saw the same pattern in our geezers—individuals who remained effective leaders even as the world changed around them. Indeed, they often seemed to become *more* effective leaders as a result of change. Existing theories of leadership based on personality traits and situational explanations simply couldn't account for the rich data in front of us. They didn't adequately explain the dynamic process that we saw again and again, in which era, individual factors, and certain key competencies—adaptive capacity, above all, but also the ability to engage others through shared meaning, voice, and integrity—coalesced around a critical experience or event to transform the individual. Why, we asked ourselves, are some people able to extract wisdom from experience while others become its victims? To answer that question, we had to propose a new theory of how leaders are made. That theory both describes and predicts who is likely to become and remain a leader, and describes the parallel process whereby individuals become lifetime learners.

We discovered the heart of that new theory as we listened to leader after leader tell us their "defining moment" stories. Each of these autobiographical tales had at its core a crucible, as we described in chapter 4. *Crucible* was the portmanteau term we needed, elastic enough to include the wide range of transformational events that our leaders experienced, from Tara Church's revelation about paper plates to Muriel Siebert's battle against the Wall Street boys club. Many of our leaders had been changed in one crucible after another. But in every case, the experience was a test and a decision point, where existing values were examined and strengthened or replaced, where alternative identities were considered and sometimes chosen, where judgment and other abilities were honed. Every crucible is an incubator for new insights, ideas, and conceptions of one's self. Often the transformational event is a traumatic one, as it routinely is in war, and it sometimes involves the daunting realization that the individual has power over other people's lives. This discovery is sobering, thrilling, and empowering, all at once. Whatever the crucible experience—going into battle, immersion in another culture, being mentored, overcoming fears—the individual created a narrative around it, a story of how he or she was challenged, met that challenge, and became a new and better self. That story is often so convincing that it inspires others to follow the narrator.

Remarkably, as we reread our growing collection of autobiographical stories, we discovered that virtually every one was about the education of the narrator. Although each of our leaders had a distinctive way of saying it, each could have described his or her life as Solon did almost 3,000 years ago when he said of himself: "Each day he grew older and learned something new." Learning how to learn may be the single greatest gift that our leaders took away from their crucibles, the all-in-one tool that they could depend on in all their subsequent dealings with other people and the world. When their having learned how to learn was combined with creativity, our leaders were unstoppable.

In the course of our interviews, we were repeatedly struck by how engaging our subjects were. This was a quality independent of their fields of endeavor and their specific achievements. Almost all were people that you wanted to spend time with. Had you met them at a party, you would have been reluctant to move on. This quality existed independently of intelligence and beauty—although many of our leaders had both—and it had nothing to do with their age. There was something else about virtually all of them that made us want to linger and hear more of what they had to say. We realized that our leaders all enrolled others in their enthusiasms. They had an aura about them, an energy.[2] Youthfulness doesn't quite describe it. We saw the signs again and again. Eyebrows raised in

wonder and surprise. An openness to experience. An unselfcon-
scious candor. A mischievous smile and contagious laugh. Wit.
Resilience. Curiosity. Tirelessness. An almost palpable hunger for
experience and an incapacity for bored detachment. These are the
winning attributes of a brilliant child, and we found them embodied in reflective, intelligent, sociable adults. We began referring to
this all-important quality—one that recruits others and lubricates
social interactions—as *neoteny*. Often confused with charisma,
neoteny, we came to see, was the almost magical quality that
draws people to our older, lifetime leaders, helping to insure that
they have a constituency and a stage.

Playing Any Song

As we spent more and more time trying to isolate the qualities
and conditions that allow some to lead for a lifetime, we were
reminded of a story—an autobiographical story not unlike the
anecdotes we plumbed our subjects for. After years of procrasti-
nation, one of us asked a piano teacher if it would be possible to
learn to play a few songs without going to the trouble of weekly
lessons and learning to read sheet music. The teacher, a shrewd
judge of character, asked why we wanted to learn "a few songs."
To fulfill a fantasy, she was told, to produce a beautiful, pleasing
sound. Frowning, she replied that, yes, one could learn a few
songs. But after a tantalizing pause, she brightened and asked,
"How would you like to play *any* song?"

Somewhere along the line, our geezers (and some of our geeks)
learned how to play any of the songs required of a leader—not
just how to manage a crisis, not just how to recruit, not just how
to articulate the vision of the organization, but all these and
more. Interestingly, when we asked our geeks and geezers to tell
us their theories of leadership, most were not especially eloquent.
But when we asked them to tell us how they handled some specific
situation requiring their leadership, they were wonderfully adept
at describing the challenge, the context, their tactics, what was at

stake, the players, and, finally, what went right, what went wrong, and what it all meant. All first-class noticers, they observed themselves as well as others. Self-reflection was clearly ingrained in them. Often, in an interview, the leader would stop him- or herself in midsentence to question something he or she had just said. The result would often be a midcourse correction. These mini-experiments in real time, which allowed the leader to change direction based on what he or she had observed, were fascinating examples of responsive leadership—and of learning— in action. Their habit of extracting lessons from every situation was obvious in how they responded to being interviewed. Our subjects were never passive. As eager to learn as to teach, they were always turning the tables on us. We were repeatedly asked what we had learned so far, how other people had answered our queries, why we asked certain questions and not others, how we would answer our own questions, and what the turning points were in *our* lives. Obviously, our interviewees had no intention of investing two or more hours of their time without learning something useful in the process.

Toward the end of the project, we tried a little experiment. Central to our study was the question: How do geeks become geezers? In the spirit of that question, each of us drew up his own list predicting which of our geeks would mature into lifetime leaders. Remarkably, we both came up with the same list of names. No exceptions. That bolstered our confidence in the reliability of our findings. So did what we were reading about adult development in the recent work of George Vaillant and others. Our confidence was reinforced further by what we saw and read about leaders in the world around us. The battered economy and the struggle with terrorism were crucibles on a global scale, and we saw daily how some leaders were forged by them, while others faltered. The media were rife with illustrations of the importance of adaptive capacity and the other leadership competencies we had identified.

From the start, we believed that whatever we discovered would have real-world applications. And we are more convinced than ever that the attributes and attitudes of our geeks and geezers will improve leadership in all the areas that matter most: in the public arena, in organizations, and in individual lives. The remaining sections in this chapter look at these practical applications and the rewards, both personal and professional, of leading for a lifetime.

Where Have All the Leaders Gone: The Case for National Service

Let's start with the macrocosm. As we said earlier, after September 11, old-fashioned heroes were newly prized, as were such long-unfashionable ideals as self-sacrifice and public service. Young and old, liberals and conservatives, the entire nation was moved to tears by the heroism of New York City firefighters, police officers, and others who raced into the blazing World Trade Center while everybody else was rushing out. The world that had been preoccupied with stock options a year earlier was suddenly filled with people eager to donate money and blood and to express both their sorrow for the victims and their new sense of patriotism. Even people jarred by the jingoistic rhetoric and the potential loss of individual freedoms in any war on terrorism found themselves stirred by images of the American flag and the largely decent, pluralistic society it represents.

While it will take years to sort out the meaning and consequences of the attacks, it has become clear that the nation, and indeed much of the world, was hungry for heroic leaders. Rudolph Giuliani's transformation overnight into "Churchill in a baseball cap," as the press dubbed him, was just one example. Whatever else the attacks did, they focused attention on the paucity of leaders worldwide, a leadership vacuum that has become painfully obvious in recent years. Throughout its history, the United States has seen wartime as an opportunity as well as a crisis. For more than six decades, American advances in science and technology have been facilitated by the vast scientific infrastructure created in preparation for World War II by Vannevar Bush and other vision-aries. The computer and the Internet are just two examples, albeit world-changing ones. World War II was also a powerful engine for economic growth and social change for a half-century or more. Whether the war on terrorism is truly a war is beside the point. It is undoubtedly a rare opportunity to school new leaders and to bring them together to identify and solve important problems. It is, in short, a crucible, and we need to recognize it as such so we can exploit it for the common good.

Shortly after the attacks, one of us was giving a talk at Williams College, where the repeated refrain of its gifted young students was, in essence, "Where do I sign up?" For the most part, these are not young men and women who would normally consider joining the military or any other restrictive organization. But the attacks made virtually everyone newly aware of the big issues that we so rarely think about in ordinary times: What would I do with my life if I had only a short time to live? What activities are wor-thy of my time? How can I best use my talents?

In the wake of the attacks, people were newly aware of them-selves as part of a larger world and eager to find a meaningful role for themselves in this changed reality. Young people not yet launched on a career and, indeed, most thoughtful people wanted to do something more than fly an American flag on the side of their car. Throughout the country, millions of people began to do all the things we now know people do in crucibles, including ques-tioning their priorities and values and weighing new alternatives.

Clearly, it is in the public interest to seize the opportunity cre-ated by these unprecedented events to enlarge our existing pool of leaders. John Gardner, one of our geezers, once observed: "When the United States had a population of three million, we fielded six world class leaders: Washington, Jefferson, Hamilton, Madison, Franklin, and Adams. Now we've got eighty times that many peo-ple. We need four-hundred eighty leaders. Where are they?" Good question, and one that could be asked by any country in the world.

Potentially, at least, they are everywhere. College students once focused on how soon they could start their dot-com have begun talking publicly about signing up for the Central Intelligence Agency. War or not, the crisis engaged the hearts and minds of many people, young and old, who suddenly wanted to serve their country in some honorable fashion. We haven't seen such an outpouring of idealism in the United States since a young President Kennedy captured the imaginations of a generation and inspired many of America's best and brightest to join the Peace Corps.

Clearly, if we want more leaders, we need to provide potential leaders with opportunities to learn and practice their craft. The attacks underscored the need for new institutions to channel and release the idealism and energy that were almost palpable, organizations that would also inevitably serve as training grounds for future leaders. The Peace Corps is one proven model. Another is Wendy Kopp's Teach For America, which trains talented, idealistic people to become teachers and elevates what is too often a hard, undervalued, underpaid job into a recognized form of public service.

Joseph Campbell once remarked, "In medieval times, as you approached the city, your eye was taken by the cathedral. Today, it's the towers of commerce. It's business, business, business."[3] When we asked our geeks to name their most admired leaders, after they cite their family members and high school coaches and some spiritual leaders and the occasional Endorser Millionaires like Michael Jordan and Tiger Woods, lo and behold, they name some Rushmorean business leaders, like Jack Welch and Bill Gates. Their responses reflect both Campbell's observations and one that is even more important: that over the past two decades, the most important and underreported story is how the market trumped politics. To paraphrase Joseph Campbell, we've become a "bottom-line" society.

Of course, all that may change as a result of September 11, 2001. Our nation's eyes, once again, are turning toward public leadership for direction and meaning, just as the geezer's era turned to Roosevelt and Churchill. Thomas Mann wrote in the middle of the last century that "In our time the destiny of man presents its meaning in political terms."[4] Perhaps one positive outcome of the

September tragedy will be a renaissance of political and public leaders setting the standard for future leadership, rather than our recent exclusive, almost obsessive, preoccupation with business leadership. The acts of terror were a reminder that we need leaders invested in national and global interests as well as corporate goals. The only way the United States will again see the likes of Washington, Lincoln, and Roosevelt is by recognizing the unique contribution of those who put more selfish concerns on hold in order to serve some larger public good. For this to happen, however, our national priorities will have to change so that we can recruit and educate the best and brightest for civic leadership.

Another "crash" became publicly visible early this year, far less graphically destructive than the two turbojets crashing into the World Trade Center, but one of enormous consequence. We're referring to the Enron crash, the most momentous and costly bankruptcy-cum-scandal in U.S. financial history. The Enron scandal, now nastily unfolding with the many hydra-heads of deceit, cover-ups, and dissembling, has led to twelve independent congressional investigations and the temporary front-page disappearance of Osama and Afghanistan. We're now witnessing a repeat of the Watergate and Iran-Contra hearings played out in pinstripes and spreadsheets. These two crashes, the World Trade Center and Enron, coterminous in time and consequence, will inevitably lead us toward a search for a freshly imagined concept of public service.

The existing options are limited. Currently, AmeriCorps is the only official, federally supported, nationwide, nonmilitary mechanism for tapping the widespread desire to serve. Begun in 1993, it is open to people of all ages and provides work in education, public safety, environmental protection, and human services. More than 200,000 people are enrolled, mentoring teenagers, renovating low-cost housing, and restoring national parks. Volunteers serve for a year, usually with nonprofit partners such as the American Red Cross, and participants receive a tiny living allowance and an education grant of $4,725.

City Year is a more narrowly focused outlet for idealism and altruism. Founded in Boston in 1988, this much smaller operation within AmeriCorps is targeted at 7- to 24-year-olds—the Tara Churches of the world. Its Web site describes the mindset of its intended audience: "Young enough to want to change the world— old enough to do it." Its stated vision: "that one day the most commonly asked question of an 18-year-old will be, 'Where are you going to do your service year?' "[5]

In light of what we have learned about geeks, this is a program with considerable appeal. It has many virtues, including working closely with corporate partners. For example, it is currently allied with Timberland, the hiking boot and outdoor gear company, to improve the Jacksonville, Florida, public schools. We were also struck by its use of community-building stories—a proven way to communicate shared meaning. In training sessions and on other occasions, participants repeat parable-like "founding stories." The City Year communal lore includes the folk tale about stone soup (in which a pot of boiling water and a stone are transformed into a delicious soup) and Robert F. Kennedy's oft-repeated observation, "Each time a man stands up for an ideal, or acts to improve the lot of others, or strikes out against injustice, he sends a tiny ripple of hope, and . . . those ripples build a current which can sweep down the mightiest walls of oppression and resistance."

In November 2001, U.S. senators John McCain (a geezer who knows much about public service) and Evan Bayh introduced a bill that would expand the existing opportunities to serve. The proposed Call to Service Act of 2001 would expand AmeriCorps fivefold, with half the new positions dedicated to homeland defense. The bill also acknowledges the vigor and altruism of people like our geezers by calling for more service opportunities for those 55 and older. One insightful provision is for a "Senior Scholarship" that rewards older volunteers who have done 500 hours of tutoring and other forms of mentoring with a $1,000 award that can be used toward the education of a child selected by the volunteer.

Undoubtedly, we would all benefit from living in a society that expects people to spend some period of time in public service, whether it is after high school or college or, since the young are not the only ones hungry to serve, following a career doing something else. Personally, we favor voluntary programs because we believe good works shouldn't be coerced. But mandatory or voluntary, such programs should be demanding enough to teach genuine skills and the lessons of discipline, loyalty, and the like learned in such time-honored crucibles as the military. During World War II, Officers Candidate Schools cranked out thousands of individuals jokingly referred to as "four-month wonders." But in fact, those short courses in leadership, along with the battlefields of Europe and the Pacific, produced the majority of the leaders who brought unprecedented prosperity and a new social justice to the United States in the second half of the twentieth century.

In addition, we need to encourage entirely new forms of service, creative responses to the urge to serve that has long been underexploited. Ours is a pluralistic society, and we could have vigorous service organizations in every flavor, from those focused on a single activity, like Habitat for Humanity, to those aimed at people with similar styles or enthusiasms. This would boost participation by recognizing individual differences. People who would rather forego public recitations of "Stone Soup" might flock to Marathoners for Art in the Schools.

We also need to recognize that service need not be performed in vast armies or with government supervision. In fact, the nation already has thousands of smallish community-based service organizations solving local problems, despite the widespread belief that we are all "bowling alone." Like many faith-based groups, these grassroots organizations already do good works and serve as colleges for leadership. They too deserve encouragement and support.

Whatever forms new service outlets take, they are all potential crucibles. Indeed, their most important function may be as recognized rites of passage, whatever the age of participants. Hopefully, they will function as places where individuals can test themselves, including their leadership skills. Ideally, they will be safe places to fail as well as succeed. Public or national service organizations should also offer a respite from the person's too-busy "real life." Instead, they should offer opportunities both for muscular altruism and taking stock, time to dream and to try out alternative ways of living. In short, they should be places to learn and grow.

Leadership in the Workplace

Our findings also have great relevance for the workplace. Most contemporary organizations give lip service to leadership development, but how many are truly committed to it? Leadership can't be taught in the occasional in-house program. It certainly can't be forged during a week in the woods spent rock climbing and bonding with fellow leaders-in-training. Even ten weeks in Harvard's Advanced Management Program is only a start. In other words, leadership training can't be an add-on. It has to be embedded in the very fiber of the organization.

Some companies do this better than others. One of Jack Welch's acts of genius was creation of the Crotonville, New York, "People Factory," where he spent at least one day a month sharing all he knew about leadership with individuals identified as having the edgy, competitive spirit that people need to succeed at General Electric. Welch understood that you have to put money behind your commitment to leadership development, and he spent 3 percent of the GE payroll annually on training and education. Intel devotes 130 employee-hours a year to leadership development and invests a record $5,000 per person per year. We already know that such investment pays off. According to a recent study of 3,000 American companies by researchers at the University of Pennsylvania, 10 percent of revenues spent on capital improvements boost productivity by 3.9 percent. A similar investment in development and human capital pushes productivity up 8.5 percent.

In order to create more leaders, corporations have to conquer their fear that they will invest in leadership training only to lose their best people to competing organizations. They will. But they will also reap the benefits of having the best people for a time and a greater chance of bringing them back in the future. Meanwhile, the company that gets serious about leadership training can guarantee that other well-equipped leaders are in the pipeline. The process has to start with recruitment and a systematic search for leadership potential in every prospective hire. Next, the organization has to make leadership training a top priority. It has to get serious about what it already knows. Everyone agrees that mentoring is a key step in creating leaders. But how many companies identify individuals who are or could be great mentors? Do you know of any company that has such a list? How much effort is put into preparing mentors to be effective, or into protégés to help them make the most of that relationship? And how much time is devoted to matching mentors with the right protégés? Organizations must also begin rewarding people on the basis of what we have learned about the alchemy of leadership. How many companies identify and reward individuals with notable adaptive capacity? How many praise—let alone reward financially—a failure that was worth trying?

Many organizations like to describe themselves as learning organizations. How many truly are? Do they recognize the importance of crucibles as occasions for the transformational learning that is essential to leadership? Do they incorporate opportunities for learning into the daily life of the organization? Do they provide leaders with the tools and the coaching required to make the most of their formative, and transforming, experiences? Companies need to encourage employees to reflect on what they are learning even as they face new challenges. Companies have to learn that quiet thoughtfulness may be more productive than frantic bustle. Employees need to be rewarded for the way they approach crises as well as for successful outcomes. Organizations also have to distinguish between the occasional good failure and habitual, unproductive failure. Employees need to be rewarded for their creativity, which inevitably means taking risks. This is always hard for organizations to do, however much they endorse it in principle. But such risk taking is essential for innovation and learning. The attitude organizations need to cultivate toward employees who take imaginative risks is that of Tom Watson, Sr., founder of IBM. Watson once had a promising young executive who succeeded in losing the company $10 million in an experiment that failed. The young man was sure Watson would fire him. "You can't be serious," Watson told him. "We've just spent ten million dollars educating you!"

One way to move companies and other institutions closer to being true learning organizations is to create a nonhierarchical culture of learning. It was regarded almost as a joke that everyone at the William Morris Agency had to start out in the mailroom, but in fact working in the mailroom meant being exposed to every department and employee in the company. What better way to get a prismatic view of the entire organization? In preparing to take over the reins of the family newspaper, former *Los Angeles Times* publisher Otis Chandler first worked in every department, doing every job from operating a press to covering a beat as a reporter. By the time he took over, Chandler had a deep understanding of the ecology of the organization and the industry as a whole. Most organizations would benefit from systematic rotation of key personnel through each and every department. A system that exposed leaders to the breadth of the organization for a sustained period of time would produce an enormous payoff—not just in familiarity with procedures, problems, and personnel but in such important, often neglected areas as enhancing the leader's empathy. Organizations also need to encourage skillful communication at every level, including responsible dissent.

In order to continue to be successful, organizations have to adapt to the changing, era-shaped needs of their workers. The longing for balance that we saw in our geeks cannot be ignored by organizations that want to benefit from their talent. An older generation of executives may dismiss the demands of younger leaders for personal time as a lack of commitment to the job. Not at all.

Employees cannot fully participate in organizational life if their most urgent needs are not being met. Downtime isn't an indulgence for our geeks. It is a necessity, part of what makes them feel whole and human.

Organizations also have to recognize that there is a developmental cycle that employees go through in the course of a career. The wise company accommodates these developmental needs. Valuable people on the verge of burnout or increasingly preoccupied with the desire to test alternative careers may need a sabbatical, an idea that most organizations resist, especially in these times of skeletal staffing. In fact, the increased demands made on today's smaller staffs may make sabbaticals more important—and more cost-effective—than ever. People's lives have trajectories that don't always match those of the organizations they are in. The smartest institutions make accommodations rather than drive good people out. The Israeli Armed Forces, for example, has been grappling recently with an outflow of able officers. As an Israeli general explained to one of us: "All they want is a couple of years off to work at a dot-com." Although armies are rarely perceived as flexible organizations, the Israeli forces are trying hard to find a way to furlough talent, instead of losing it.

The process that creates leaders and habitual learners cannot be limited to a small group of employees. Every meeting should become a potential crucible, an opportunity for learning and change. Unless the dynamics of leadership are understood and implemented throughout the organization, the inevitable frustrations of organizational life are bound to become even more vexing.

A handful of organizations are taking leadership development seriously, meaning that they are drilling into the organizational culture activities that are "organic." "Action learning" is an example where teams of individuals, often drawn from different and diverse disciplines, work together to solve a real-life problem facing the organization or to create a new initiative. Organizational "training camps," like GE's "People Factory" at Crotonville, are often useful, and, it's worth repeating, are organic— integral to the strategic goals of the organization. But all too often, despite its trendiness, leadership development—when it is even considered worthy of attention—relies on the occasional "off-site" with opportunities for golf, spousal seminars, and hot-shot guru entertainers. They are often gorgeously expensive anodynes, a kind of microwave strategy to develop McLeaders. The long-term effects are close to minimal and can be dangerous. Leadership doesn't have a systematic theology, but if it did, one article of faith would be: It's a sin to put changed people back into an unchanged organization.

What about the Individual?

The model of leadership that we propose is also a theory of adult learning and development. Finding ways to live well grows ever more important as our life expectancies increase. Although some boomers are notoriously reluctant to face it, the prospect of a longer life increases the potential for suffering as well as joy.

What does our model tell us about both leading and living well? Both require learning how to learn. All our geeks and geezers devised their own learning strategies, applying their creativity to finding new ones at each new stage in their lives. Dee Hock made sure he would never stop learning by refusing to be in any organization or institution that tried to blunt, control, or direct his curious mind. Sidney Harman and many of our other geezers are voracious readers and systematic collectors of interesting people, another sure way to learn. When Elizabeth McCormack flew with a particularly wise colleague, she would look over his shoulder to see what he was reading, an excellent strategy for updating your reading list. As we have said before, successfully navigating one of life's crucibles arms you for the next. If one source of wisdom and comfort failed our leaders, they found another—that's what those with adaptive capacity always do. Thus, when McCormack's husband's hearing began to fail, they read more and listened to their beloved music less.

For lifetime leaders, learning is as natural as breathing. They squeeze all they can out of every new acquaintance and encounter. They regard life's sterner, less pleasant side as a particularly instructive classroom. Arthur Levitt, who often enjoyed the perquisites of power, was also in publishing where, he recalls, "I had to sit outside a space buyer's offices and endure the humiliation that one endures when you are trying to hustle business. That was a learning experience as well." In that unprivileged position, Levitt learned always to return phone calls—everyone's phone calls, not just those of the elite. "It's so easy to do," Levitt points out. "And it makes such a lasting impression." Don Gevirtz revealed that he had learned an enormous amount from a painful divorce. Everything our leaders learn, including the sting of failure, gets added to their tool kits.

Another strategy our leaders use is to learn from other generations. Our geezers cultivate younger friends and unselfconsciously learn from their children and grandchildren. They also seek out wise older friends because they know that the crucibles of aging face all of us. Our geezers understand, as we all should, that the successful old can lead the way as we deal with the inevitable challenge of finding an exciting, useful, healthful place in a culture that continues to despise and fear old age.

Building and maintaining networks across generations, organizations, and cultures is a way to learn continuously and to leverage the insights of people who have a genuine interest in your growth and success. For example, several geeks we interviewed talked about having their own personal "boards of directors"— people whose opinions they valued who could be called upon as a source of information and/or a reality check. These networks have, in several instances, proven invaluable to individuals who found themselves confronting difficult ethical and moral situations which they knew they could not solve alone. Because of their networks, they had a richer variety of actions available to them; moreover, they did not have to face their situations alone.

One of the heartening messages sent by all our geeks and geezers is that taking risks has enormous rewards. Geeks like Jeff Wilke routinely push themselves outside their comfort zones. Ian Clarke said he always tries to put himself in situations that test him. When he was younger, he told us, he always wanted bigger feet. He had a theory that if he bought shoes a size too large, he would grow into them. "I always place myself in a situation that I'm not quite equipped to deal with, but I learn," Clarke said. "That's how I do it . . . I buy one shoe size bigger than I actually need and grow into it." Our geezers are inveterate risk-takers, willing to fail spectacularly because the payoff in education is so great.

Our leaders are not so focused on the future that they don't take care of the mundane business of staying well. Almost to a person, our geezers are physically active. Think of Frank Gehry on his skates and Arthur Levitt happily trouncing his young wife on the tennis court. They do so because they understand the health benefits of exercise and of engagement. Most of our geezers seemed to be just hypochondriacal enough to stay on top of their physical health but not to the point of obsession. None of our successful geeks or geezers is socially isolated. All are part of a large network or networks of family, friends, and acquaintances. At the same time, all our geezers are comfortable spending contemplative time alone.

Almost every one of our geezers announced at some point in his or her interview that they believed they were lucky. They were certain that they would succeed in the future as they had so often in the past. They had, in short, the life-enhancing gift of optimism even in hard times. They also showed no evidence, at least to us, of bitterness about people who might have harmed them in the past. It was clear that they looked to the past only when we asked them to do so. Their preferred orientation was to what was happening now and what would happen tomorrow. They expected good things.

Of course, luck favors those who are prepared, and for the lifelong leaders we studied, practice is an essential element of preparation. Like doctors, lawyers, and artists, they view their craft as something that unfolds, changes, and improves over time. They practice their craft all the time. But practice does not mean "artificial" or "not real" in the sense that a teacher might give a child a practice exam that "doesn't count." Instead, practice is an organic part of the task—neither less important than performance nor estranged from it. Unlike many busy managers and executives who claim that they don't have time to practice because they must perform all the time, these leaders have learned to *practice while they perform.*

Anyone who masters a musical instrument, golf, chess, magic, or public speaking has had the "out of body" experience of observing themselves while they perform, noting opportunities for improvement or innovation as they perform, and carrying out adjustments— even experimenting with entirely new behaviors— on the fly. This supplements traditional forms of practice (e.g., hours repeating basic moves, scales, swings, gestures). In fact, a good performance demonstrates the value of practice. Practice and performance come to be viewed as inseparable: There is no practice without implications for performance and no performance without reflection on practice.

The key to practicing in the midst of performance is to identify where opportunities exist—or can be created—in the context of everyday performance and make them your practice field. Find ways to notice yourself in action, to experiment with different ways of behaving in real time, and to adjust your behavior based on those real-time micro-experiments. Don't wait for "retreats" and "time-outs" to engage in reflection and learning. Watch yourself on videotape—in both formal and informal settings, as many of our geeks and geezers do—to see yourself as others see you. Engage the people you work with as observers; give the ones you trust permission to draw attention to words, phrases, and actions that contradict or undermine goals you want to achieve. Periodically test your understanding of a situation by sharing it with others.

Practicing while you perform also prepares you to recognize when you are in the midst of a crucible, or about to enter one, and what your options are in dealing with it. Edgar Allan Poe, in his powerful short story "Descent into the Maelstrom," describes how, in the midst of chaos and uncertainty, some people achieve a clarity of mind, an elemental calm that enables them to see things happening around them that others cannot see or refuse to see. Those who become adept at practicing while they perform experience a similar calm and clarity. They learn to extract wisdom from experience. They find in that calm the courage to enter new crucibles.

The idea of "practicing while you perform," if not identical to, certainly resonates with our earlier point about integrating leadership development into the everydayness of organizational life. Crucibles do not have to be created. They exist in real time, everywhere and all the time. Boring meetings. Unspoken grievances. Closed doors. Unexplained actions. Undeployed talents. Subtle rejections. The "little murders" that deplete energy and lower self-esteem. Belief systems that require questioning, dozing like sacred cows. We're talking about the mundane, the quotidian problems of everyday life. There are untapped crucibles that, unless used as laboratories for organizational learning, ossify into bad practices. These are the crucibles that all organizations, to a greater or lesser extent, try vainly to conceal but are manifestly expressed in dysfunctional and destructive actions. The irony is that these "sleeping viruses," these unnoticed crucibles, are the most potent and useful opportunities for learning to lead. Organizations as well as individuals must learn to identify such crucibles and to leap in.

One adjustment that we were especially interested in was how longtime leaders dealt with the loss of power. Almost all our geezers continued to take active roles in the public arena. Some, such as Gehry, had more clout at 70 than they had ever had before. But the few who were no longer heading important institutions or making decisions with wide impact had found new outlets for their energy and other gifts. Many were devoting more time to mentoring. A number were engaged in a kind of wholesale mentoring by writing memoirs. The adaptive capacity of our subjects occasionally reminded us of the resilience evidenced by Jimmy Carter, who reinvented himself as a leader of enormous moral power after a relatively unsuccessful presidency. Whether our geezers were in the public eye or not, they sought out crucibles at every turn. They reflexively looked for the take-home lesson in every new experience, even unpleasant ones like surgeries. They all talked excitedly about the latest thing they had learned, and, neotenics all, their eyes were still full of wonder.

As we were readying our manuscript for publication, we came across a gem of geezer wisdom from no less an authority than Edith Wharton. "In spite of illness," she wrote, "in spite even of the arch-enemy, sorrow, one can remain alive long past the usual date of disintegration if one is unafraid of change, insatiable in intellectual curiosity, interested in big things, and happy in small ways."[6] Words to live and grow by, whatever your age.

Biographies

Geezers

Warren G. Bennis (March 8, 1925)

Distinguished Professor of Business Administration and founding chairman of the Leadership Institute at the University of Southern California, Warren Bennis is a prolific writer, consultant, and speaker on the topic of leadership. Over his forty-five-year career, he has authored or edited more than twenty-seven books and 2,000 articles, including the best-sellers *Leaders* and *On Becoming a Leader,* and has advised four U.S. presidents. Bennis, who has a Ph.D. in economics and social science from MIT, served on the faculties of MIT, Harvard, and Boston University and was president of the University of Cincinnati from 1971 to 1977. One of Bennis's most cherished accomplishments is, at 19, serving as one of the youngest infantry commanders in Europe during World War II and earning the Bronze Star and Purple Heart.

John Brademas (March 2, 1927)

President Emeritus of New York University, John Brademas has dedicated his life to public service. He is a graduate of Harvard and was a Rhodes scholar, earning his Ph.D. at Oxford. First elected to the United States House of Representatives at 31, he represented his home state of Indiana for twenty-two years, serving as House Majority Whip his last four years. In Congress, he focused much of his attention on the arts and education. After serving in Congress, Brademas stayed involved in education, serving as president of New York University from 1981 to 1992. He led NYU's transformation into a major national and international research university. He also served as chairman of the Federal Reserve Bank of New York, the National Endowment for Democracy, and by appointment of President Clinton, of the President's Committee on the Arts and the Humanities. He currently sits on several corporate and nonprofit boards.

Jack Coleman (June 24, 1921)

Most recently owner and editor of a weekly newspaper in Chester, Vermont, Jack Coleman was raised in a small smelter town in northern Ontario, Canada. A former Haverford College president, he has led an interesting and varied career. Coleman began his career as a professor at MIT after receiving a Ph.D. in economics from the University of Chicago. He later taught at Carnegie Mellon, served as chairman of the Federal Reserve Bank of Philadelphia, and was the director of the Edna McConnell Clark Foundation. As president of Haverford, he used his sabbaticals to perform blue-collar jobs, working as a garbage collector, dishwasher, and prison guard. He later spent ten days living as a homeless person on the streets of New York and also served as an auxiliary New York City policeman.

Robert L. Crandall (December 6, 1935)

Currently active on a variety of corporate boards, Bob Crandall retired in 1998 as CEO and chairman of the board of AMR (American Airlines), having served as its president since 1980. He graduated from the University of Rhode Island and the University of Pennsylvania's Wharton Business School. Prior to joining American in 1973, Crandall held jobs with Kodak, Hallmark, and TWA. He successfully led American through the postderegulation airline era, instituting "super-saver" fares and the first frequent-flier program, and expanding American's reach to Europe, Asia, and South America. He is credited with transforming American Airlines into one of the world's leading airlines.

Father Robert F. Drinan, S.J. (November 15, 1920)

A Jesuit priest for over fifty years, Father Robert Drinan has been active in both government and education. He spent ten years in the United States House of Representatives representing the suburbs of his native Boston, having first run for the Congress in response to his opposition to the Vietnam War. Formerly the dean of Boston College Law School, Father Drinan has served on the faculty at the Georgetown University Law Center since 1981. He has been an outspoken advocate for many human rights causes, has served on numerous committees related to these causes, and has written extensively on the subject.

Robert Galvin (October 9, 1922)

Recently retired as chairman of the executive committee of Motorola, Robert Galvin had served the company founded by his father since 1940. The longtime chief executive of Motorola, he was first elected president in 1956 and stepped down as chairman of the board in 1990, exactly fifty years to the day he started at the company. Galvin expanded Motorola's reach worldwide and consistently updated its mix of products to remain at the fore-front of new communications and electronics technologies. His grandson, Brian Sullivan, was also interviewed for this book.

John Gardner (October 8, 1912–February 16, 2002)

A consulting professor at Stanford at the time of his death in 2002, John Gardner dedicated much of his life to public service. He has worked both in government, as secretary of the Department of Health, Education and Welfare under Lyndon Johnson, and in community service, as head of the National Urban Coalition and the founder of Common Cause. A noted author on community and leadership, his books include *Self-Renewal* (1964, 1981) and *On Leadership* (1990). Gardner received an A.B. from Stanford and a Ph.D. in psychology from the University of California at Berkeley before serving as a Marine intelligence officer during World War II. Gardner also served on the boards of numerous corporations and nonprofit institutions.

Frank Gehry (February 28, 1929)

Born in Toronto, Canada, Frank Gehry is a world-renowned architect perhaps best known for his design of the Guggenheim Museum in Bilbao, Spain. He was educated at the University of Southern California and then at Harvard; he established his first architecture practice in 1962 in California. His buildings have been referred to as being more like functional sculptures. He has been awarded the Gold Medal from the American Institute of Architects and the Pritzker Prize, considered the top award in the architecture field. Gehry still enjoys playing hockey.

Don Gevirtz (March 1, 1928–April 22, 2001)

Raised in Kokomo, Indiana, Don Gevirtz attended the University of Southern California on a basketball scholarship prior to embarking on a successful business and public service career. He cofounded the Foothill Group, which grew to become one of the nation's largest commercial finance companies and was later sold to Wells Fargo. Heavily involved in politics, Gevirtz served as U.S. ambassador to Fiji from 1996 to 1997. He was active in supporting improvements in education, and much of his philanthropy was focused at the Graduate School of Education at the University of California, Santa Barbara. Gevirtz passed away in April 2001 at the age of 73.

Edwin Guthman (August 11, 1919)

Born in Seattle, Washington, Edwin Guthman has been one of the nation's leading journalists for the past fifty years and a journalism professor at USC since 1987. He began his newspaper career in Seattle after being awarded the Silver Star and Purple Heart during World War II. He won a Pulitzer Prize at age 29 and later served as press secretary to Attorney General Robert Kennedy. After leaving Washington, he was the national editor of the *Los Angeles Times* from 1965 to 1977 and then the editor of the *Philadelphia Inquirer* from 1977 to 1987. Guthman was featured in Tom Brokaw's book *The Greatest Generation*.

Sidney Harman (1920)

Cofounder in 1953 and chairman and CEO of what is now Harman International, Sidney Harman has been a pioneer in the audio field for fifty years. Harman has built the company he began by selling products out of the back of his car into the world's premier high-end audio company, with over $1.6 billion in sales during fiscal year 2000. Harman has taken a great interest in and written extensively about the quality of working life and the conditions in his factories. He served the Carter administration as deputy secretary of commerce during 1977 and 1978 and currently sits on a variety of boards of nonprofit organizations.

Frances Hesselbein

Frances Hesselbein was the founding president and CEO of the Peter F. Drucker Foundation for Nonprofit Management from 1990 to 1998 and now serves as the chair of its Board of Governors. Recognized as one of America's most successful businesswomen, she is probably best known for her leadership as CEO of the Girl Scouts of America of the U.S.A. from 1976 through 1990. She is editor-in-chief of *Leader to Leader,* a quarterly leadership journal, and serves on many nonprofit and corporate boards. In 1998 she received the Presidential Medal of Freedom, which is America's highest civilian honor.

Dee Hock (March 21, 1929)

Born in small-town Utah, Visa founder and CEO emeritus Dee Hock started the credit card company in 1970. Originally founded as Visa U.S.A., Visa International followed in 1974 as a decentralized, nonstock company owned by financial institutions around the world. He left Visa in 1984 and has since focused his thought and research on management practices and the evolution of institutions. He is the author of *Birth of the Chaordic Age* and founder and director of the Chaordic Alliance.

Nathaniel R. Jones (May 13, 1926)

Born in Youngstown, Ohio, U.S. Court of Appeals Judge Nathaniel Jones has worked tirelessly for the cause of civil rights throughout his legal career. He grew up economically disadvantaged but thrived under the guidance of his mentor, local lawyer and newspaperman J. Maynard Dickerson. After serving in the Army Air Corps during World War II, he was one of only two African-Americans in his law school class at Youngstown State. Judge Jones was appointed assistant U.S. attorney in Ohio in 1961. He later served as general counsel for the NAACP from 1969 to 1979, prior to being nominated to the federal bench by

President Carter in 1979. He has since served on the U.S. Court of Appeals for the Sixth Circuit, assuming senior status in 1995.

Arthur Levitt, Jr. (February 3, 1931)

Born in Brooklyn, New York, Arthur Levitt, Jr., has led a distinguished business career, rising to become the longest serving head of the U.S. Securities and Exchange Commission from 1993 to 2001. At the SEC, his top priority was the protection of individual investors. Levitt graduated Phi Beta Kappa from Williams College in 1952 and then spent two years in the Air Force. After that, he began his wide-ranging business career, which included working for *Life* magazine and a cattle company before moving to the brokerage business. He was formerly chairman of the American Stock Exchange and owned Capitol Hill's *Roll Call* magazine immediately prior to being appointed by President Clinton to head the SEC.

Elizabeth McCormack (March 7, 1922)

A former nun, school headmistress, university president, and now chairman of the Board of Trustees of the Population Council, Elizabeth McCormack has spent a lifetime involved in education and public service. As a nun in the Order of the Sacred Heart for thirty years (she left the order in 1974), McCormack focused her life work on education, first as a teacher and headmistress, and later as president of Manhattanville College from 1966 to 1974. After leaving Manhattanville, she went to work running the Rockefeller family philanthropic office, from which she retired in 1989. She has served on a variety of boards, including the board of the MacArthur Foundation.

Bill Porter (November 10, 1928)

Bill Porter, the founder and chairman emeritus of E*Trade, was born in Boulder, Colorado. After serving in the Navy, getting a B.A. at Adams State, and earning a master's at Kansas State, Porter joined the Bureau of Standards, and later General Electric. He is the holder of fourteen different patents and is responsible for numerous innovations and inventions throughout his career. Porter founded E*Trade in 1982, and the company placed the first on-line trade in July 1983. The company went public in 1996. Porter and his wife Joan have been heavily involved with MIT, the school where Porter received his M.B.A. in 1967.

Ned Regan (May 30, 1930)

Ned Regan has led a distinguished career in public service and education. Born in 1930, Regan served in the Korean War and was first elected to the Buffalo City Council in 1964. He continued in elected office and eventually served fourteen years as the New York State comptroller, where he was responsible for New York's financial management and its state pension fund. In July 2000, at the age of seventy, he became president of New York City's Baruch College, a 15,000-student business college in the City University of New York (CUNY) system.

Richard Riordan (May 1, 1930)

Born in New York and educated at Princeton, Richard Riordan is best known as the former mayor of Los Angeles. He stepped down in July 2001 after serving two full terms. Riordan is a lawyer with a J.D. from the University of Michigan and had a law practice in Los Angeles prior to becoming mayor in 1993. He has also been a successful entrepreneur and venture capitalist. As mayor, he focused on public safety, education, and the improvement of the neighborhoods of Los Angeles. Riordan still plays hockey with another one of our interviewees, Frank Gehry.

Sidney Rittenberg (August 14, 1921)

Author of *The Man Who Stayed Behind*, Sidney Rittenberg, who was educated at the University of North Carolina at Chapel

Hill and Stanford, spent almost thirty-five years living in China. He learned Chinese in the military and began living in China after World War II, at first working mainly as a translator. He was admitted to the Chinese Communist Party in 1946 and later spent a total of sixteen years in Chinese prisons in solitary confinement. He was first jailed after the Soviet Union accused him of spying and later jailed for speaking out against the government in the wake of the Cultural Revolution. He returned to the United States in 1980 and has since continued his work of strengthening ties between the U.S. and China.

Muriel Siebert (September 12, 1932)

Muriel "Mickie" Siebert is one of the leading women of Wall Street, and in fact was the first woman to own a seat on the New York Stock Exchange. She is the founder of the discount broker-age firm that bears her name. She worked successfully for a number of different securities firms prior to purchasing, at great difficulty, her seat on the NYSE in 1967. She was appointed and served as New York State Banking Commissioner for five years beginning in 1977. Still active in business, Ms. Siebert devotes much of her time to charity and a wide range of nonprofit organizations.

Paolo Soleri (June 21, 1919)

Born in Turin, Italy, noted designer and architect Paolo Soleri first came to the United States in 1947 to study under Frank Lloyd Wright. Settling in the United States for good in 1956, Soleri, who first gained fame as a ceramicist, has since devoted most of his energies toward urban planning. His major work has been Arcosanti, a prototypical town designed by Soleri in central Arizona. The town is designed according to Soleri's concept of "arcology," which combines architecture with ecology and maximizes the interaction between people while reducing pollution and the use of raw materials.

Walter Sondheim, Jr. (July 25, 1908)

Still active in public service, Walter Sondheim, Jr. has been one of Baltimore's most revered citizens for the past half-century. Formerly an executive with the Hochschild, Kohn department stores, Sondheim retired from the business in 1970 and has since focused his efforts on civic service in Baltimore. As far back as 1954, Sondheim, then president of the Baltimore City School Board, successfully led Baltimore schools through integration in the aftermath of the *Brown v. Board of Education* decision. He was also a guiding force in the development of Baltimore's Inner Harbor, which revitalized the downtown area. Sondheim is a graduate of Haverford College.

Mike Wallace (May 9, 1918)

Born five doors down from John F. Kennedy in Brookline, Massachusetts, Mike Wallace has been a fixture on the CBS news program *60 Minutes* since its inception in 1968. Wallace's broadcasting career began in radio in 1939 upon his graduation from the University of Michigan. Through his work on *60 Minutes,* Wallace, still engaged and excited by his work into his eighties, has helped pioneer and define the field of investigative journalism. He has interviewed and reported on all of the important newsmakers of our recent history. During World War II, Wallace served as a naval communications officer.

John Wooden (October 14, 1910)

Born in rural Indiana, legendary basketball coach John Wooden spent twenty-seven years as head coach of UCLA. Since his retirement from coaching in 1975, Wooden has been a noted lecturer and requested speaker, often discussing his theory on success, the Pyramid of Success. His teams' ten NCAA championships, including seven consecutive titles, are unrivaled, but it is Wooden's role as teacher-coach that makes him a fascinating leader. A 1932 graduate of Purdue University, Wooden received the Big Ten Medal given to the graduating athlete with the highest grade-point average. Wooden has been inducted into the Basketball Hall of Fame as both a coach and a player.

Geeks

Elizabeth Altman (December 16, 1966)

Liz Altman is vice president and director, Business Development, Personal Communications Sector, for Motorola. A graduate of Cornell with a master's in Mechanical Engineering and a master's in Management from MIT's Leaders for Manufacturing Program, Altman joined Motorola in 1992. She spent two years at Polaroid between her academic stints at Cornell and MIT. While at Motorola, Altman received a fellowship through the U.S. Department of Commerce and spent a year working at a Sony factory in Japan. She serves on the board of the Japan Society of Boston and is active at Cornell, serving on the President's Council of Cornell Women.

Lorig Charkoudian (February 14, 1973)

Lorig Charkoudian founded and is the executive director of the Baltimore Community Mediation Program. A 1995 graduate of Pomona College, Charkoudian received a Ph.D. in economics from Johns Hopkins in 2001. The goal of the Community Mediation Program is to empower residents to resolve disputes nonviolently. The program was originally started in the Waverly/Greenmount area of Baltimore, but has now expanded to cover the entire city. She is also active in running nonviolence workshops in prisons and has campaigned against the death penalty. Charkoudian serves on the board of various nonprofit agencies.

Steve Chen (June 6, 1969)

Steve Chen cofounded Embark.com, a provider of Internet infrastructure solutions to students, high schools and colleges, and related businesses. Over 600 higher education institutions are using Embark.com management tools. Chen has served as vice president of sales. Prior to founding Embark.com, Chen worked at Mecon, a start-up health care information services company, and before that, worked in consulting. He received his undergraduate and graduate degrees from the Massachusetts Institute of Technology.

Tara Church (March 6, 1979)

In 1987, at the age of 8, Tara Church founded the Tree Musketeers as the first known U.S. nonprofit agency actually administered by kids. Tree Musketeers is committed to empowering young people to lead environmental and social change. Its chief focus has been on planting trees and educating young people about the environment. Church's vision is that individuals can make a difference, and at Tree Musketeers, with its focus on tree planting, each child can feel like he or she is actually doing something to improve the environment. Church graduated from the University of Southern California in 2000, and is now a student at Harvard Law School.

Ian Clarke (February 16, 1977)

Ian Clarke was born in Ireland and is a 1999 graduate of the University of Edinburgh, Scotland, with a degree in computer science and artificial intelligence. He is best known as the founder of Freenet, an open source peer-to-peer network that encourages the free exchange of information while ensuring confidentiality. An anticensorship advocate, Clarke is also a founder of Uprizer, Inc., an Internet infrastructure company whose technology is based on the architecture of Freenet.

Dan Cunningham (June 19, 1975)

A 1997 graduate of Princeton University, Dan Cunningham is on his way to becoming a serial entrepreneur. Founder and CEO, or "Chief Chokolada," at Dan's Chocolates, an on-line retailer of fresh chocolates, Cunningham's previous start-up, sportscape.com, is now part of on-line sports retailer Fogdog. His first company was a lawnmowing company he started in high school in his native Vermont. Dan's Chocolates' concept is to deliver fresh, high-quality handmade chocolates while contributing 5 percent of revenues to the charity of the customer's choice.

Sky Dayton (August 8, 1971)

Founder of Earthlink and Boingo Wireless, as well as cofounder of eCompanies, Sky Dayton was introduced to computers by his grandfather in 1980, at age 9, and has since been fascinated with technology. In 1993, after being frustrated in his attempts to log on to the Internet, Dayton decided there needed to be an easier way to get on-line, and Earthlink was born. In June of 1999, he became a cofounder of eCompanies, an Internet incubator based in Santa Monica, California. In late 2001, he founded Boingo Wireless. In what little free time he has, Dayton is an avid snowboarder and surfer.

Harlan Hugh (February 19, 1974)

At age 6, Harlan Hugh began working with his father's Apple II computer, and his fascination with computers and technology still drives him today. Hugh invented the technology behind and cofounded The Brain Technologies Corporation. The technology behind The Brain provides a platform for sharing and organizing information, and the company's mission is "to help people turn their existing information into knowledge." Hugh has brought in a seasoned management team to help him run the company's operations, and he remains chief technology officer.

Elizabeth Kao (July 18, 1968)

A graduate of the University of Texas and MIT's Leaders for Manufacturing Program at the Sloan School of Management, Elizabeth Kao is now a marketing manager at Ford. Kao cofounded her own firm between her undergraduate years at Texas and earning her master's and M.B.A. from MIT. At Ford, Kao has held positions in both manufacturing and marketing, giving her a perspective on multiple aspects of Ford's business.

Geoffrey Keighley (June 24, 1978)

A 2001 graduate of the University of Southern California and a native of Toronto, Canada, Geoffrey Keighley has been writing video game reviews since he was 13. Keighley was always ahead of the curve in terms of technology, using early forms of e-mail to communicate with video game makers. Originally a video game beta tester, he has evolved into one of the industry's foremost writers and reviewers. In 1996, Keighley founded and is now editor-in-chief of Gameslice, a video game industry Web site that goes beyond the typical video game reviews and instead focuses on more in-depth features, editorials, and interviews.

Michael Klein (December 3, 1970)

A college student at age 14 and a self-made millionaire before 20, Michael Klein has been a leading entrepreneur for almost fifteen years. His grandfather Max, creator of the 1950s phenomenon Paint by Numbers, introduced him to business at a young age. After first making it big in the real estate industry after college (he was 17), Klein got into the software industry. He was founder of Transoft, acquired by Hewlett Packard in 1999, and CEO of eGroups, a free group e-mail service that was acquired by Yahoo! for $432 million in 2000. Klein, who holds an M.B.A. and a J.D., now has a young family.

Wendy Kopp (June 29, 1969)

Wendy Kopp used her senior thesis at Princeton to develop the concept behind and found Teach For America, a program that trains and puts top college graduates in teaching positions in underprivileged areas. Teach For America was founded immediately after Kopp's 1990 graduation from Princeton, and in 1990, the first group of 500 teachers was in the field. Just over ten years later, there are 1,500 top college grads teaching over 100,000 children in fifteen underprivileged urban and rural locations. Kopp is still running the program, and in 2001 authored *One Day, All Children . . . : The Unlikely Triumph of Teach For America and What I Learned Along the Way,* a book chronicling the first ten years of the Teach For America program.

Brian Morris (January 30, 1971)

Born in Baltimore, Brian Morris is the founder of Legacy Unlimited, LLC, a Baltimore-based provider of financial education, products, and services to previously underserved minority communities. Prior to founding Legacy, Morris worked for Legg Mason and Merrill Lynch after graduating from the University of Maryland. He was appointed by the mayor and served as Baltimore's first director of minority business development. In 1998, *Ebony* magazine recognized Morris as one of the nation's top leaders under age 30.

Lingyun Shao (August 27, 1977)

A 2000 graduate of MIT, Lingyun Shao was already a sergeant in the U.S. Army and a licensed nurse by the time she graduated from college. She was recently voted one of the top ten college women in the United States by *Glamour* magazine. While in the Army Reserves she served as a nurse in rural El Salvador during relief efforts after Hurricane Mitch and also worked as a nurse at Massachusetts

General Hospital. Although she would like to become a doctor, Shao envisions having a number of different careers.

Young Shin (July 9, 1966)

A cofounder of Embark.com, Young Shin most recently served as the company's president and CEO. In his new role as chairman and chief technology officer, he focuses on enhancing the company's product vision, strategy, and architecture. Prior to founding the company, Young was the director of information technology for Mecon, a health care information services company. Before Mecon, he directed the application architecture practice at Seer Technologies' Consulting division. He graduated from Massachusetts Institute of Technology and the Sloan School of Management with dual degrees in Aeronautical and Astronautical Engineering and Management Science.

Bridget Smith (July 31, 1978)

Born in New York City and a graduate of Brooklyn Technical High School and Wellesley College, Bridget Smith was awarded a Truman Scholarship in recognition for her leadership and public service. After Wellesley, she enrolled at Harvard's Kennedy School of Government and then University of California at Berkeley Law School. The daughter of an Irish mother and an African/American Indian father, Smith is interested in change to improve the lives of America's children. Much of her volunteer work has involved inner-city communities, and she has been a member of AmeriCorps.

Brian Sullivan (October 8, 1971)

Grandson of "geezer" Robert Galvin, Brian Sullivan is president, chief executive officer, and founder of Rolling Oaks Enterprises, a venture capital and bridge financing firm. Rolling Oaks was

founded in 1998 and focuses its funding on early-stage information technology companies. Sullivan received a B.S. in communications from Northwestern University and an M.B.A. from the
University of Southern California. Robert Galvin serves on Rolling
Oaks's Board of Advisors.

Jeff Wilke (December 23, 1966)

A graduate of Princeton University with an M.S. in chemical
engineering and an M.B.A. from MIT's Leaders for Manufacturing
Program, Jeff Wilke is a senior vice president and general manager
of worldwide operations and customer service for Amazon.com.
At Amazon, his operational responsibilities have included working on their vital distribution and logistics strategy. Prior to moving to Amazon, Wilke was in senior management at Allied Signal;
he worked for Andersen Consulting (now Accenture) before
going to MIT for business school. A native of Pittsburgh, Wilke,
his wife Lisel, and their two daughters are now enjoying the West
Coast life.

Interview Questions

I. Life Line

Instructions: Draw a line on a sheet of paper that begins with your birth and ends at a point ten years past your current age. On that line, place an "x" at the points in your life that to you represent major turning points in defining who you are.

What are those defining moments? Why did you choose them?

What role has failure played in your life?

Do you feel lucky?

II. Leadership

What are your first memories of being a leader?

How would you describe yourself as a leader?

How has your leadership style changed?

How good a follower are you? Whom do you follow?

Whom do you admire? What historical or contemporary world figure would you like to sit next to for ten hours on a plane?

[Tell the story of Ed (CEO) and Jim (young man leaving Ed's company). What might Ed have said/done to change Jim's mind?]

III. Success

How do you define success? How did you define it age 30? How will you define it at age 70?

How long do you expect to stay in your current position?

How many organizations do you expect to work for in your career?

When do you expect to retire?

Where in the U.S. would you least like to live? What job would entice you to live there?

What makes you happy?

IV. Meaning/Life Space

Instructions: Consider for a moment the things that matter to you most in your life right now. How would you allocate 100% among those things in order of their importance to you right now?

To 30-year-olds: How would the allocation look when you're 70?

To 70-year-olds: How did the allocation look when you were 30?

Where do you go to get inspiration?

When you are in crisis, where do you go to get advice?

What differences do you see between your generation and your children's generation? Your parent's generation?

What do you want to leave as a legacy?

How important is your mental and physical condition?

What are you doing to grow? How do you measure it?

Do you feel your work and nonwork life is in balance?

V. Fill-In Questions

To me, the essence of leadership is _____

A perfect day for me is _____

I tend to learn best when _____

My personal hero(es) is (are) _____

My favorite work of fiction _____

My favorite work of nonfiction _____

Age _____

Gender _____

Race/ethnicity _____

Marital status _____

Education (degree and field) _____

Birthplace _____

Current residence _____

Current employer _____

Title _____

Years in current position _____

NOTES

FOREWORD

1. David McCullough, "Harry S. Truman," in *Character Above All: Ten Presidents from FDR to George Bush,* ed. Robert A. Wilson (New York: Simon and Schuster, 1995).

2. Ibid.

3. Dean Keith Simonton, *Greatness: Who Makes History and Why* (New York: Guilford Press, 1994).

CHAPTER 1

1. E. B. White, *Charlotte's Web* (New York: HarperCollins, 1952).

2. Readers can view excerpts from several of the interviews by visiting our Web site: http://www.geeksandgeezers.com.

3. Warren Bennis and Patricia W. Biederman, *Organizing Genius: The Secrets of Creative Collaboration* (Cambridge, MA: Perseus, 1998).

4. Karl Weick, "Legitimization of Doubt," in *The Future of Leadership,* ed. Warren Bennis, Gretchen Schweitzer, and Thomas Cummings (San Francisco: Jossey-Bass, 2001).

5. The senior Klein was a classic American entrepreneur of his generation who had left an unsatisfying job with General Motors to strike out on his own. As the owner of the Palmer Paint Co. in Detroit, he applied the assembly-line methods he learned in auto-making to his factory, but his chief assets were the drive and imagination that were unleashed when he left his corporate job. Always looking for new markets for his product, Klein immediately saw the potential when the head of his art department, Dan Robbins, proposed

a do-it-yourself kit that would allow amateurs to create professional-looking paintings. Robbins had borrowed the idea from Leonardo Da Vinci, who numbered the different areas of his paintings so his assistants would know what colors to use. Klein made the crucial decision to nix the abstract contemporary designs that Robbins originally proposed in favor of landscapes, bull-fights, kittens, and other subjects that appealed to buyers in America's burgeoning suburbs. The subject of an exhibit at the Smithsonian in 2001, the resultant paint-by-number phenomenon made history.

6. Vernon E. Jordan, Jr., and Annette Gordon-Reed, *Vernon Can Read! A Memoir* (New York: Public Affairs Press, 2001).

7. Ibid., 9.

8. Edwin Markham, "Outwitted," in Cary Nelson, ed., *Anthology of Modern American Poetry* (Oxford: Oxford University Press, 2000).

9. Dave Smith and Walt Disney, *The Quotable Walt Disney* (New York: Hyperion, 2001).

CHAPTER 2

1. In Ralph Keyes, *The Wit and Wisdom of Harry Truman: A Treasury of Quotations, Anecdotes, and Observations* (New York: Random House, 1999).

2. *Life* magazine, 31 July 1950.

3. Jean-Paul Sartre quoted in David Caute, *The Great Fear: The Anti-Communist Purges under Truman and Eisenhower* (New York: Simon and Schuster, 1978).

4. William H. Whyte, *Organization Man* (New York: Simon and Schuster, 1956).

5. Cited in Eugenia Kaledin, *Daily Life in the United States: 1940–1959* (Westport, CT: Greenwood Press, 2000).

6. Desi Arnaz paraphrased in Kaledin, *Daily Life in the United States*, 134.

7. According to the Gallup Index of Leading Religious Indicators, 55 percent of Americans in 1996 said that religion was very important in their lives versus 75 percent in 1952, <http://gallup.com/poll/indicators/indreligion.asp> (accessed 15 November 2000).

8. Whittaker Chambers, *Witness* (New York: Random House, 1952), 9.

9. "Heroes and Icons," *Time*, 14 June 1999.

10. Philip E. Slater, "Leading Yourself," in *The Future of Leadership: Today's Top Leadership Thinkers Speak to Tomorrow's Leaders*, ed. Warren Bennis, Gretchen M. Spreitzer, and Thomas G. Cummings (San Francisco: Jossey-Bass, 2001).

11. Life expectancy for a white male in the United States at the time most geezers in this study were born (around 1925) was 59 years. So, if you were conditioned from youth to think you'd live to be 60 or 65, then many geezers were understandably thinking that they'd reached the midpoint of life before 35. By contrast, when the geeks were growing up, life expectancy had extended to 73 and the idea of mortality had not been cemented as early as it had been for geezers.

12. William Strauss and Neil Howe, *Generations: The History of America's Future, 1584 to 2069* (New York: William Morrow, 1992), 272.

13. David Halberstam, *The Best and The Brightest* (New York: Fawcett, 1993).

14. Secretary of Labor Elaine Chao gave the issue a personal touch in an April 2001 interview: "In a stressed-out work force, people are concerned about balancing personal life versus professional lives, and I think that technology is a big part of that as well. It's supposed to help us, yet how many of us are now beset by ringing cell phones and laptops that accompany us on weekends and on our vacations so that we're never away from the workplace? I mean, I'll get up at two o'clock in the morning and dash off a couple of e-mails, and I think that's crazy!" National Public Radio, Morning Edition, 4 April 2001 (transcribed from Web archives).

15. Douglas McGregor, *The Human Side of Enterprise* (New York: McGraw-Hill, 1960).

CHAPTER 3

1. Moore's Law was the observation made in 1965 by Gordon Moore, cofounder of Intel, that the number of transistors per square inch on integrated circuits had doubled every year since the integrated circuit was invented. Moore predicted that this trend would continue for the foreseeable future. In subsequent years, the pace slowed down a bit, but data density has doubled approximately every eighteen months, and this is the current definition of Moore's Law, which Moore himself has blessed. Most experts, including Moore himself, expect Moore's Law to hold for at least another two decades.

2. Apple's employment offer: "Here's the deal Apple will give you; here's what we want from you. We're going to give you a really neat trip while you're here. We're going to teach you stuff you couldn't learn anywhere else. In return . . . we expect you to work like hell, buy the vision as long as you're here. . . . We're not interested in employing you for a lifetime, but that's not the way we are thinking about this. It's a good opportunity for both of us that is probably finite," cited in Peter Cappelli, *The New Deal at*

Work: Managing the Market-Driven Workforce (Cambridge, MA: Harvard Business School Press, 1999), 25–26.

3. Neil Howe and William Strauss, "The New Generation Gap," *The Atlantic Monthly*, December 1992.

4. Andrew Hultkrans, "GenXploitation," *Mondo 2000*, December 1992.

5. Eric Schmitt, "For First Time, Nuclear Families Drop Below 25% of Households," *New York Times*, 15 May 2001.

6. Marc Gunther "God and Business," *Fortune*, 19 July 2001.

7. Note also that before you could play most board games you—or your parents—first had to wade through a complicated instruction manual. Today, by contrast, players just launch the game. They assume that game developers have created an intuitive, learn-as-you-play interface.

8. Paolo Soleri, an internationally renowned urban architect and philosopher, quietly shook his head sadly when we asked him what he thought about the ambitions of young men and women in 2001. According to Soleri: "[T]his notion that the child is a genius and you're going to become whatever you want to become is such a cruel insult. . . . Because life is not that. Life is a harsh reality. And we have to find our way into this harsh reality without fooling ourselves. So all those potential presidents of the United States, 275 million of them, it's so cruel."

9. Abby Ellin, "Have Your Freedom Now, or Later?" *New York Times*, 15 July 2001.

10. The other movies were *Wall Street, American Beauty, Good Will Hunting,* and *Swingers.*

11. According to studies cited in Robert Reich, *The Future of Success* (New York: Knopf, 2001), in 1970 less than 40 percent of female college graduates married to male college graduates were in the workforce. Now, nearly 75 percent of those women earn a paycheck.

12. Sally Jacobs, "In a League of Her Own: Princeton's First Female President," *Boston Globe*, 10 July 2001.

13. This mirrors the results of a Web-based survey of young people reported by the *Wall Street Journal* (27 June 2001): 38 percent of the 12,000+ respondents chose heroes from their families.

CHAPTER 4

1. Our thinking in this chapter has been very much influenced by a cadre of gifted authors to whom we want to acknowledge our debt: Albert Bandura, *Self-Efficacy: The Exercise of Control* (New York: Freeman, 1997); Jerome Bruner, *Acts of Meaning* (Cambridge, MA: Harvard University Press, 1990); M. Csikszentmihalyi, *The Evolving Self* (New York: HarperCollins,

1993); Howard Gardner, *The Mind's New Science: A History of the Cognitive Revolution* (New York: Basic Books, 1985); Daniel Goleman, *Working with Emotional Intelligence* (New York: Bantam Books, 1998); K. Gergen and K. Davis, *The Social Construction of the Person* (New York: Springer-Verlag, 1985); Robert Kegan, *In Over Our Heads: The Mental Demands of Modern Life* (Cambridge, MA: Harvard University Press, 1994); and Karl Weick, *Sensemaking in Organizations* (Thousand Oaks, CA: Sage 1995).

2. George E. Vaillant, *Adaptation to Life,* (Cambridge, MA: Harvard University Press, 1995).

3. George E. Vaillant, *Aging Well: Surprising Guideposts to a Happier Life from the Landmark Harvard Study of Adult Development* (New York: Little Brown, 2002).

4. Aldous Huxley, *The Perennial Philosophy* (New York: Harper-Collins, 1990).

5. Vaillant, *Aging Well,* 9.

6. John McCain with Mark Salter, *Faith of My Fathers* (New York: Random House, 1999).

7. Quoted in "Personal Histories: Leaders Remember the Moments and People that Shaped Them," *Harvard Business Review* 79, no. 11 (December 2001): 30–32.

8. Diana E. Henriques and Jennifer Lee, "Flinty Bond Trader Leads His Firm Out of the Rubble," *New York Times,* 15 September 2001.

9. John Keats, "Letter to George and Tom Keats (December 27, 1817)," in *Letters of John Keats,* ed. Robert Gittings (Oxford: Oxford University Press, 1970).

10. "Personal Histories," 32.

11. Isabel Allende, *Paula* (New York: HarperCollins, 1996).

CHAPTER 5

1. Frank Rich, "The Father Figure," *New York Times Magazine,* 30 September 2001.

2. Gerald Posner, "I Was Wrong About Bush," *Wall Street Journal,* 25 September 2001.

3. Ibid.

4. Leo Braudy, *The Frenzy of Renown: Fame and Its History* (New York: Vintage, 1997).

5. D. T. Max, "The Making of the Speech," *New York Times Magazine,* 2 October 2001, 32ff.

6. Drake Beam Morin Consulting Co., Inc., "CEO Turnover and Job Security: A Special Research Report" (Boston: Drake Beam Morin, 1999), 6.

7. Saul Bellow, *Ravelstein* (New York: Penguin, 2001).

8. "New Formula: To Fix Coca-Cola, Daft Sets Out To Get Relationships Right," *Wall Street Journal*, 23 June 2000, 1.

9. "The Year in Business," *Fortune*, 24 December 2001, 142.

10. Leslie Kaufman, "Question of Style in Warnaco's Fall," *New York Times*, 6 May 2001.

11. Richard Finneran (ed.), *The Collected Poems of W.B. Yeats* (New York: Scribner, 1996).

12. William James, *The Letters of William James, Volume 1* (New York: Longmans Green, 1878).

13. C. Wright Mills, *The Sociological Imagination* (New York: Oxford University Press, 1959), 165–194.

14. Derived from Warren Bennis and Patricia Ward Biederman, *Organizing Genius* (Reading, MA: Addison-Wesley, 1997), 172.

15. William James, *The Letters of William James*.

16. F. O. Mathiessen and K. B. Murdock, *Notebooks of Henry James*, (New York: Oxford University Press, 1961).

17. George E. Vaillant, *Adaptation to Life* (Cambridge, MA: Harvard University Press, 1995), 120.

CHAPTER 6

1. T. H. White, *The Once and Future King* (New York: Putnam Publishing Group, 1980).

2. "If personality is an unbroken series of successful gestures, then there was something gorgeous about him, some heightened sensitivity to the promises of life, as if he were related to one of those intricate machines that register earthquakes ten thousand miles away." F. Scott Fitzgerald, *The Great Gatsby* (New York: Charles Scribner's Sons, 1925).

3. From an unpublished speech.

4. Cited in Kenneth Minogue, *Politics: A Very Short Introduction* (London: Oxford University Press, 2000).

5. See <http://www.americorps.org>.

6. Edith Wharton, *The Age of Innocence* (New York: Modern, 1999).

INDEX

reading habits of, 175
on success, 40
McGrath, Russell, 40
McGregor, Douglas, 48
meaning
  creating from crucible experience,
    17–18
  making/finding, 4–5, 107–108
  shared, 121, 134–137, 138
mentors/mentoring
  bonding as form of, 152–153
  finding, 104
  Klein's, 119
  relationships with protégés, 16
Merrill, Charles, 60
metaphors of different eras, 12.
    See also neoteny
middle-class society, 27–29
military service, 27, 34–35, 48
Mills, C. Wright, 147
Milton Bradley Company, 31
Moore's Law, 53–54
moral choices, 144–145
moral compass, 145–146, 148,
    149
Morris, Brian, 60, 61, 106, 195
Moscone, Diana, xx
Mother Theresa, 148

Naked and the Dead, The (Mailer),
    24
Nasser, Jacques, 74
national service, 165–171
negative capability, 101
neoteny, 20–21, 119–120, 150–153,
    163
networking, 68, 176
1990s era, 55–57
Nohria, Nitin, xix

nurturing response in humans,
    151–152

Odyssey, The, 16
Once and Future King, The
    (White), 157
OODA (observe, orient, decide,
    and act), 83
Oppenheimer, J. Robert, 122,
    148
opportunity, 102, 103
optimism, 19, 177
ordeals, transforming, 14–16, 96.
    See also crucibles
Organization Man era, 25–27,
    27–29, 37, 54
Organization Man (Whyte), 68
*Organizing Genius: The Secrets of
    Creative Collaboration* (Bennis
    and Biederman), 9
Orwell, George, 99

Parker, Dorothy, 43
participative management, 115
Patterson, Neal, 132–133
paying your dues, 37–41
Peace Corps, 167
personal wealth, 59, 60–62
Pfeiffer, Eckhard, 131–132
Pius XII, Pope, 25
Poe, Edgar Allan, 178–179
politics as entertainment, 53
Porter, Bill, 39
  on criticism of big companies,
    36–37
  on getting ahead, 35–36
  on opportunity, 102
Posner, Gerald, 125

Warren G. Bennis is University Professor and Founding Chairman of the Leadership Institute at the University of Southern California. He is Chairman of the Center for Public Leadership at Harvard's Kennedy School and the Thomas S. Murphy Distinguished Research Fellow at the Harvard Business School. He has been on the faculties of MIT, Boston University, INSEAD, IMD, and the Indian Institute of Management at Calcutta. He has served as Provost of the State University of New York at Buffalo and President of the University of Cincinnati. He is also a consultant for many Fortune 500 companies and has served on four U.S. Presidential Commissions.

Referred to as the "Dean of leadership gurus" by *Forbes* magazine, Bennis has written twenty-seven books on leadership, change, and creative collaboration. The *Financial Times* recently named Bennis as the person who established leadership as an academic discipline. One of his books, *Leaders*, was recently designated as one of the top fifty business books of all time. Another, *An Invented Life*, was nominated for a Pulitzer Prize. He has still to fulfill one of his lifelong dreams: to write a terrific one-act play.

Robert J. Thomas is a Senior Research Fellow with Accenture's Institute for Strategic Change in Cambridge, Massachusetts, and an Associate Partner specializing in the area of leadership and transformational change. He has consulted to a wide variety of global companies in the fields of leadership development, organization design, and implementation of new technology. Thomas is also a senior lecturer at the MIT School of Engineering. Before joining Accenture, Thomas taught on the faculties of the University of Michigan and MIT's Sloan School of Management for thirteen years.

Thomas has authored four books and numerous articles on leadership, technology, and organizational change. His book *What Machines Can't Do: Politics and Technology in the Industrial Enterprise* was the winner of the 1995 C. Wright Mills Award. He is currently at work on two new books, *Crucibles for Leaders* and *Launching a Successful Campaign Strategy for Change*.